The GIRLFRIENDS GUIDE BOOK

The GIRLFRIENDS GUIDE BOOK

NAVIGATING FEMALE FRIENDSHIPS

marian jordan

B&H
PUBLISHING GROUP

NASHVILLE, TENNESSEE

978-0-8054-4673-9

Published by B&H Publishing Group

Nashville, Tennessee

Dewey Decimal Classification: 177

Subject Heading: WOMEN \ FRIENDSHIP \

CHRISTIAN LIFE

1 2 3 4 5 6 7 8 • 15 14 13 12 11

Contents

"As iron sharpens iron, so one *woman* sharpens another."
(Proverbs 27:17)

Dedicated to
Leti Lusk, Leigh Kohler, and Susannah Baker . . .
Our years of accountability taught me
the meaning of Proverbs 27:17. I am forever
grateful for your friendship.

Warning: A Travel Advisory

While putting the finishing touches on this book, I was simultaneously booking airline tickets for a ministry trip that would literally take me around the globe: *Houston to New York, New York to Mumbai, Mumbai to Hong Kong, Hong Kong to Seoul, Seoul to Frankfurt, and finally, Frankfurt to home.* Whew! Jet lag anyone?

After purchasing the tickets, a travel advisory issued by the US government concerning a few places on my tour posted to my in-box. Nothing major—just run-of-the-mill State Department warnings. As a good citizen, I clicked through the e-mail, noting the various vaccine requirements and terror alerts that have now become standard fare for those of us who brave the "friendly skies."

Closing the e-mail, my mind naturally drifted to this book. As I thought of all the various issues and topics raised concerning our female friendships, I thought to myself, *I suppose it would only be fair of me to give a travel advisory of my own. Girls need to be warned of a dangerous temptation they will face while reading this book.*

While this warning is not from the State Department, and I certainly don't require the measles vaccine for my readers, I do, however, have an important caution before you journey into *The Girlfriends Guidebook*: Please read this book for yourself . . . *not for your girlfriends*! What I mean by this, of course, is that we must fight the temptation to think, *Ooh, I sure wish my friend would read this book. She definitely has some major emotional baggage.*

Please fight the urge to mail an anonymous copy to her with certain sections dog-eared and highlighted! My intention in writing *The Girlfriends Guidebook* is to grow deeper friendships built on honesty and love—not to divide friendships through anger and resentment . . . and a few not-so-subtle hints.

In the course of this book, you will explore God's design for friendship, as well as unpack the baggage that results from living in a sinful and fallen world. Do yourself and your friends a favor: Please don't finger-point or fault find. Instead, allow God's Word to speak to *you*, about *your* heart, and to show *you* where *you* need to mature. Trust me, it is oh-so-easy to recognize if a friend is failing but oh- so-easy to forget how often you and I fall short too.

I say all this, of course, as a girl who has personally walked this journey. I couldn't write this book without first living every word of it. I know the struggles women deal with in friendships. None of us are immune to envy, jealousy, and insecurities galore. As I've studied God's Word, this experience has been more than research; it has been transformational. God has revealed *my* junk, *my* insecurities, *my* baggage, and areas in *my* life that need to mature. I certainly have a long way to go, but I pray with Christ's help I will be a better friend today than I was when I started this journey.

My prayer is that God uses *The Girlfriends Guidebook* to expand your vision for the beautiful gift of friendship. I pray you won't miss out on one single breathtaking moment He has designed for you. Ultimately, I pray you fall more in love with Jesus, the best friend a girl could ever have, and in the end you reflect *His* love more and more.

CHAPTER 1

The Girlfriends Guidebook

Lost. Confused. Totally, completely, ridiculously off course.

My girlfriends and I wandered back and forth through the corridors of Venice for hours, and still we were going around in circles. Every turn opened into a new alleyway that led to a different fork that led to another nook and cranny of the majestic city still undiscovered. Time flew by, of course, as we were distracted by the business of window-shopping, photo-snapping, and pastry-tasting.

By the end of the day, we were clueless as to how to get back to our hotel, nor did we know the address, and the sun was rapidly setting. We assumed that we'd just find our way back. Boy, were we wrong. At that point a little bit of fear began to set in.

I kicked myself for leaving my *Rick Steve's Guide to Italy* back in our hotel room. I sure could have used a handy dandy guide right about then—an instruction manual with a cute little pull-out map and tips pointing out the "must see" spots in each city. It's helpful too, of course, that my friend Rick also warns gullible blonde travelers like me of the tourist traps to avoid. I'm a BIG fan of guidebooks. Stacked in a corner of my library are travel guides from destinations all over the world, and I would have given anything to have one on hand when I was lost in Venice.

When four of my girlfriends and I decided to backpack Europe together, we had no idea of the adventures that awaited us: the strangers we'd meet on the trains, the views that literally took our breath away, or the countless cathedrals and museums we'd visit. Not to mention that we also managed to visit every gelato shop on the European continent. (I highly recommend wild berry, but I digress.)

To this day, we still laugh with tears rolling down our cheeks at memories from that trip. But one moment we will never forget is the day we managed to get lost in Venice. I'm just sayin', Venice is confusing—bridges, gondolas, crazy Italian men chasing you down the avenue yelling, "Bella, Bella." It all looks the same . . . but at the same time *different*. Without a map, without a guidebook, it was difficult to navigate the twists and turns of a city set on water.

Venice is also remembered as the breaking point in our little party of five. We were halfway through our journey, and our feet were blistered from running through train stations, our backpacks were growing heavier with every new purchase, and our patience was being tested by each of our five strong personalities. Our relationships were feeling the pressure. Mix a few controlling personalities (ahem, yours truly) in with multiple hurt feelings, misunderstandings, short fuses, growing tensions over schedules, low blood sugar, unspoken expectations, and jet lag; and, well, you get a situation ripe to expose what is inside individuals. And let's face it, what comes out of us in those moments is not always so pretty: jealousy, competition, control, anger, manipulation, and resentment, just to name a few less-than-cuddly aspects of our personalities.

The sad truth is my friends and I are committed followers of Jesus. Each one of us loves Jesus and desires more than anything to live for His glory. But in that moment we weren't representing Him very well. In fact, in that kind of moment—and sometimes in other moments—we are mostly concerned with getting our way or improving a circumstance we don't like. Relationships, even among committed Christians, can be tough sometimes.

During a particularly tense time in the day, I thought to myself, *A girl could really use some sort of guidebook for navigating her female friendships.*

For instance . . .

- What am I supposed to do when my friend is giving me the silent treatment and I don't know why?
- How am I supposed to react when it feels like middle school, and I'm the girl not picked to sit at the lunch table?

- Should I just ignore the fact that we always do what she wants to do?
- Why do I get so irritated when she says that?
- Why do I feel so taken advantage of, hurt, and frustrated?
- Am I secretly starring as a contestant on *Survivor*?

Just think about it: We have all these books on dating, marriage, raising kids—every topic under the sun—but how many books tell us what to do when you feel hurt by a girlfriend? Where is the guide that tells you what to do when your best friend walks away? Where do you turn to learn how to be a better friend when you've blown it in the past? And what about jealousy, competition, drama, or the hurt you experience when a friend gets married, gets pregnant, or moves away?

Thankfully our group made it through Venice in one piece—physically and emotionally. We finally found our way back to the hotel, and with a few humble apologies we found our way back into one another's good graces. But I know plenty of examples where the friendship didn't survive the rough patch. In researching for this book, I've heard hundreds of heartbreaking stories from women of all ages describing the pain and disappointment they've felt as a result of a broken friendship. I definitely have my own tales of friend-shifts, "frenemy" relationships, and friend-breaks.

While I can say wholeheartedly that friendship is an

amazing gift from God, I must also confess that some of the most painful tears I've ever cried and some of the hardest roads I've ever walked have been because of my female friendships. I know I'm not alone. As I travel and minister to women across the nation, I've heard stories of confusion and disappointment from women regarding their friendships. Questions abound and the pain is real. We have legitimate struggles in our relationships that need to be addressed. Ignoring the issues doesn't help. I know this from experience.

This journey that we call friendship is a road marked by both mountaintops and valleys, winding curves and confusing detours; but the journey is worth it. Over the years I've seen new friendships flourish into lifelong relationships and others end with unspoken pain and bitterness. Through it all I've seen the hand of God moving.

The gift of friendship has a divine purpose. The Giver of the gift uses His blessing for a far greater purpose than either party can foresee. As we take this journey together, I pray you will discover the depths of God's purpose for your friendships and apply the truth found in His Guidebook to build relationships that glorify

> *T*his journey that we call friendship is a road marked by both mountaintops and valleys, winding curves, and confusing detours; but the journey is worth it.

Jesus and truly stand the test of time. Honestly, we all need a few pointers from time to time when it comes to our female friendships. Here are three important reasons:

1. Our Culture

First of all, we live in a culture that makes an absolute mockery of the word *friend*. Few people actually know what that word means anymore. Take for instance the onslaught of social media such as Facebook. These mediums give us the impression that a "friend" could be a perfect stranger who just happens to click your name on a computer screen. When in actuality, a friend—according to the Bible—is someone who "sticks closer than a brother" and "would lay down his life for you" (Prov. 18:24 and John 15:13, author paraphrase).

Another cause of confusion is how friendship is depicted by reality television. A few years ago MTV catapulted a few normal California high school girls into global stardom when they created the TV series *Laguna Beach*. This series followed a group of girls and depicted the drama of their "friendships." High school graduation didn't end the spotlight for these girls . . . oh no; it only paved the way for the drama-filled cat-fighting-friend-feud we call *The Hills*. Each season of *The Hills* highlighted cattiness, gossip, name-calling, envy, jealousy, and competition for boy attention. The saddest thing was that the word *friend* was thrown around as a meaningless title. These girls used and abused one another and did little justice to the true meaning of friendship. Relationships between the lead characters would start and end within a thirty-minute episode. What's the result? Young women today are left with the impression that a friend is expendable, that relationships are based on "what you can get" instead of on sacrificial love for another, and that lying, backstabbing, gossiping, and drama are just normal girl behavior.

Lest we believe that friend troubles are strictly limited to those in middle school, high school, or college, think again. The corporate world is not a cakewalk for female relationships. So-called "friends" can turn on one another in a hot second if it means gaining advancement in a career. And one of the stickiest seasons for women can be the mommy stage of life. My married friends confess to me feelings of insecurity, jealousy, and competition that arise in their friend groups.

Hollywood puts this drama on a supercharged level with reality TV shows like *The Real Housewives of Orange County* or *New Jersey*. Once again we see women who use the term *friend* to describe their relationships, yet their actions are far from friendly most of the time.

Scripture describes our modern-day culture perfectly in 2 Timothy 3:1–5:

"Don't be naive. There are difficult times ahead. As the end approaches, people are going to be self-absorbed, money-hungry, self-promoting, stuck-up, profane, contemptuous of parents, crude, coarse, dog-eat-dog, unbending, slanderers, impulsively wild, savage, cynical, treacherous, ruthless, bloated windbags, addicted to lust, and allergic to God. They'll make a show of religion, but behind the scenes they're animals. Stay clear of these people." (*The Message*)

In a day and age when selfishness reigns supreme, true friendship is rarely seen. We desperately need to reexamine what it really means to be a friend.

2. Our Calling

You are the light of the world. A city on a hill cannot be hidden. Neither do people light a lamp and put it under a bowl. Instead they put it on its stand, and it gives light to everyone in the house. In the same way, let your light shine before men, that they may see your good deeds and praise your Father in heaven. (Matt. 5:14–16 NIV)

Of all the places I've visited in the world, nowhere on earth compares with Israel. I love God's Word, and the Bible absolutely comes alive when you walk where Jesus walked, stand on the hillside where He taught, sail in a boat on the very waters that He calmed with just a word, and see the landscape He used so often to illustrate His teachings.

I'll never forget standing by the shore of the Sea of

Galilee at dusk. A calm fell on the water, and the sky transformed from brilliant blue to orange to a haze of purple as darkness fell around me. After the sun made its final bow and ducked behind the curtain of horizon, I looked up and noticed the first flicker of lights in the distance. I hadn't noticed the small village nestled in the mountainside overlooking the sea while it was daytime, but when night came, the city lights shone bright in the distance. Watching the light break through the darkness, I remembered Jesus' words, "A city on a hill cannot be hidden" (Matt. 5:14 NIV).

One of the primary reasons we need a guidebook is due to our calling as believers—to shine brightly as lights in the darkness for God's glory. As Christians, we are held to a higher standard. Jesus declares that we are "the light of the world." This means that in the midst of a world filled with selfishness, pride, division, and cattiness, a woman who is a follower of Jesus Christ must choose to go against the tide of culture. She must embrace the forgotten virtues of love, loyalty, forgiveness, and humility.

Here's the beauty of our calling: Jesus enables us to live it out. The crux of the Christian faith lies in the fact that through Jesus we are reconciled to God the Father. With sin, the great divider, destroyed at the cross, our greatest need—a relationship with God—is restored. Unlike the world that clamors for hope and seeks life in empty places, we have the true source of hope and life in Jesus.

Springing forth from our relationship with God is our ability to love and relate to others as God intended. Sin keeps a soul locked in a prison of selfishness. Jesus unlocks the cell and invites us to share in His life, enabling us to love in His power. Therefore, a woman who knows Jesus should interact in her relationships differently from those who don't know Jesus.

Every aspect of our lives should serve as a witness to Him. When we choose to gossip or betray, we tarnish the name of Jesus. When we choose to nurse a grudge or harbor unforgiveness, we call into question the power of God in us. We are called to light up the darkness so that those still in the dark may see the Light, Jesus Christ, and may also experience forgiveness and restoration. In essence, we are to be "walking billboards" for the glory of God, as explained by author and speaker Gary Thomas in his book, *Holy Available*: "When we allow God to mark our manner, alter our attitudes, and burnish our behavior, people will naturally ask, 'What is it about him? What is it about her?' They'll take note that we have been with Jesus—and have undergone dramatic change. This gives glory to God as we

> *S*pringing forth from our relationship with God is our ability to love and relate to others as God intended.

become walking billboards that proclaim his reality and redeeming power."[1]

Just imagine the impact that a woman could have in her school or community if she determined to follow Christ's example instead of the one seen on *Gossip Girl* or *Desperate Housewives*. There is something compelling about love lived out. When the world sees Christlike love in action, then the world is drawn to Him. This is our calling, and this is also why it is imperative that we address the issues that keep us from shining brightly for God's glory. For this reason, we will look closely at common conflicts that divide and destroy friendships, we will examine Scripture and discover the character qualities of a Christlike friend, and we will prayerfully transform more into His image.

3. Our Hearts

My question was simple: "Have you ever been hurt or betrayed by a friend?" Nothing prepared me for the flood of responses that filled my inbox after posting it online. Women across the country are heartbroken over rifts, misunderstandings, and betrayals. Yet for the most part we don't discuss our pain. Unlike a breakup with a boyfriend or a family quarrel, friendship struggles are swept under the rug, trivialized, or ignored. We have this idea stuck in our heads that friendships are always supposed to be easy, never complicated, and only a really messed-up person would have a friendship struggle. The reality? Friendships can be challenging, and like any damaged relationship they need healing. In the place where a welcome sign once stood, there is now a wall separating close friends; where secrets were once shared, now silence rules the day; and where there was once laughter and joy, there are now hard hearts and restless fears.

We have this idea stuck in our heads that friendships are always supposed to be easy. Friendships can be challenging, and like any damaged relationship they need healing.

Here's just a sampling of e-mails sent to me after I posted the question on Facebook. As you will see, women of all ages and stages of life have experienced hurt and live with unhealed wounds from broken friendships.

It is almost impossible for me to trust girls, I really just expect to be hurt and I don't trust them. It's easier to just hang out with guys. —Kristen, age 20

I don't want to walk through the pain of losing a friend ever again. I can't do it. Not again. That was one of the loneliest years of my life. I've never cried as much as I did over the loss of my best friend. We were very close; she was the one I talked to about everything, like a sister. So the rift in our friendship led me to a season of wrestling with grieving, hurt, bitterness, anger, and betrayal. —Amy, age 32

A woman I considered a very close friend suddenly dropped me as a friend. Not only did she drop me, she tried taking down several of my other relationships in the process by destroying my character to them. When I called to ask her if I had done anything in particular, and if so I was truly sorry, she covered the situation in niceness and exclaimed that we had just grown apart. I was devastated, especially when we shared the same group of friends and even the same mentor. I would see her everywhere I went and always felt a sense of deep rejection. Not to mention the fact that I knew I was being talked about. One person mentioned in confidence some things that this girl had said about me and I was so, so hurt. I would painfully realize that my former friend dealt with a serious case of jealousy. Sadly, I would also find out that I wasn't the only one left in her dysfunctional relational path. —Stacy, age 42

Often I will very unnecessarily and excessively read into things said or done by my friends, assuming they are mad at me, or getting ready to abandon me . . . just like my last friends. For example, if one of my friends is in a bad mood, I automatically assume she's mad at me and I go through my day trying to fix the imagined issue.

I know, this is crazy! I really struggle with thinking that my friends will walk out the door. —Debra, age 40

One of the most difficult hurts I experienced in a female friendship involved a boy (of course). I was in college at the time and had recently ended a long-distance relationship that left me heartbroken. It took a very long time to heal, and even though he lived far away, cutting ties was hard but clearly necessary. During this time, one of my closest friends moved to the city in which he lived. It didn't take long before they were "best friends." Again, my heart was crushed. I thought it was an obvious girlfriend rule that you never become close to your bestie's ex. I mean, right?? I tried to be cool, to give them the benefit of the doubt, but it was so hurtful and felt incredibly insensitive. I eventually told my friend how hard it was for me to hear about their friendship. She acted like she understood, but instead of changing her relationship with him, she just stopped telling me about it. I was totally baffled at how that could be justified on either end, but I could do nothing about it. I chose to remain friends with her, but it was very hard for almost two years. I continued being honest with her about how I felt, even confessed feelings of tension and jealousy and apologized when I felt it necessary. —Jenny, age 28

I'm sure we can all relate to these stories on some level. We need a guidebook to address the issues that divide us and one to show us how to heal the wounds inside us. Not only do we need to look at the cause of our hurt and find our way back into healed relationships, but also we need to learn how to respond to others' wounds as Christ would.

God's Word, Our Guide

Over the years I've had my own ups and downs with girlfriends. God has used these relationship issues to send me running to Him for direction, and along the way I've discovered we do have an incredible instruction manual— the Bible. God's Word is our source of wisdom and direction, and through it, He teaches us how to navigate our female friendships.

Before moving on, I want to stop on this journey and point out a few amazing things about our Guidebook. First, Scripture teaches us that "all Scripture is inspired by God and is profitable for teaching, for rebuking, for correcting, for training in righteousness" (2 Tim. 3:16). Wow! Just think about that truth for a minute—our Guidebook is "inspired by God."[2]

Women today have so many options of where to turn for wisdom in relationships—pop psychology, therapists, television talk-show hosts, women's magazines, other friends (who, frankly, don't always give the best advice), and self-help books—but do these sources actually guide us in the direction we need to go?

When turning to the Bible, we receive guidance from God. He is, after all, our Creator and Designer—the One who formed our minds and hearts and knows specifically how each one of us is wired (Ps. 139). Only God can teach us how to navigate our troubled relationships. Think about it this way, if the hard drive of my MacBook crashes, I am going directly to the Genius Bar at the Apple store. There's no point wasting time trying to fix things myself when I have a direct line to the authority.

Next, I must point out that God's Word is alive. As Hebrews 4:12 declares,

> The word of God is living and effective and sharper than any double-edged sword, penetrating as far as the separation of soul and spirit, joints and marrow. It is able to judge the ideas and thoughts of the heart.

I absolutely love this aspect of Scripture. I can't tell you the number of times I've been in the midst of a situation and a verse just pops into mind, giving me the direction I need in that moment. For example, this morning a close friend of mine called and cancelled our lunch date . . . for the *third* time in a row. Just as I was tempted to get my feelings hurt and put up a wall in our friendship, Jesus' words, "Do unto others as you would have them do unto you" (Matt. 7:12, author paraphrase) came to mind.

What's my point? The truth is I am the queen of overbooking my schedule, and on many occasions my friends extended grace to me when I forget appointments. So when my friend missed our lunch date, God reminded me that I need to give her the same grace I want to receive from others. The Bible is alive! Our Guidebook isn't an archaic history book; it is a fresh message from God to us for today.

Finally, look back at Hebrews 4:12 and notice that the Bible is "able to judge ideas and thoughts of the heart." We will dig into this aspect of Scripture in greater detail in later chapters, but for now I want you to recognize that most of us don't see ourselves clearly. We are not aware of *why* we *act* and *react* in the ways that we do. We don't recognize our true intentions. For instance:

- Why do we pull away when we feel hurt?
- Why do we avoid someone we used to spend time with on a regular basis?
- What is the real reason we feel jealous or envious?
- Or better yet, why do we really find it so difficult to trust?

As we dig into our Guidebook, we will discover the answers to these questions because God's Word will reveal to us the intentions of our hearts—why we do what we do.

Bottom line—we need help! As Christian women, our friendships should be different. Ours should be marked by both love and maturity. After all, we have the Spirit of Christ living within us, and His Word as our guide. The world is watching. If our female relationships are riddled with jealousy, backstabbing, and fighting, then our testimonies will suffer.

The goal of *The Girlfriends Guidebook* is to examine friendship from the perspective of God's Word. Unlike a human guide who can lead us off course, we have direction from God Himself, the One who not only made us and understands us but also *is* love and who formed friendships to reflect His relational nature. As we explore this topic, we will answer some important questions:

- Why does God give us friends?
- What glorious purpose is He accomplishing in these relationships?
- What does a biblical friendship look like?
- How does God use our female friendships to make us more like Christ?
- How, according to God's Word, can we become better friends to others?
- What does the Bible teach us about forgiveness and reconciliation?
- When are boundaries needed, and when do we carry our friend's baggage?

THE GIRLFRIENDS GUIDEBOOK

- How can we further the kingdom of God through our friendships?

Girlfriends, grab those travel-sized toiletries and dig out your passport, it is time for this journey to begin. Pack light and don't forget your camera—an adventure awaits us!

Friendship is the greatest of worldly goods.
Certainly to me it is the chief happiness of life.
If I had to give a piece of advice to a young man
about a place to live, I think I should say, "Sacrifice
almost everything to live where you can be near your
friends." I know I am very fortunate in that respect.

—C. S. Lewis from *The Letters of C. S. Lewis*,
December 1935

CHAPTER 2

The Destination: God's Purpose for Friendship

Here's a little fact about yours truly you might have picked up from the previous chapter, but I think would be good to declare once for all: I'm quite the globe-trotter. Not the basketball kind, of course. Actually, I am a total waste of my five-foot-eleven inches. Even with all this height, I can't dribble a basketball. That being said, my particular brand of globe-trotting is limited to international travel. I'm a girl with a passport on standby at all times just in case an exciting adventure should present itself. One of my favorite things about a new travel experience is researching a region, a country, or a city before stepping foot on the soil. I absolutely love to know the history, culture, food, quirks, and must-see spots. Armed with the right information, a huge pile of rocks transforms into the mythical Stonehenge in a flash.

A few summers ago I traveled throughout England while studying abroad at Oxford University. What made the experience so rich was the fact that I L-O-V-E all things British. Just give me a Jane Austen book and a good cup of English breakfast tea, and I'm one happy girl. And here's a side note of embarrassing proportions. When I was in fourth grade, I competed in a little local beauty pageant. (Please insert your own eye roll.) When the judges asked the contestants who they wanted to be when they grew up, I replied, quite seriously, "Margaret Thatcher." Of course, I didn't give one of the usual ten-year-old replies of "a mommy, a teacher, or a Hollywood star." Oh no! I wanted to be the female prime minister of Great Britain. I have no idea when my obsession with England began, but I can tell you one thing, it was early. Needless to say, when I set out on my summer abroad, I dove into my research with gusto, consulting a variety of guidebooks about the United Kingdom.

I prided myself on picking up the vernacular, learning how to "mind the gap," "form a queue," and order my tea with "two lumps" like a local. Once again my penchant for a good guidebook saved the day in London while traversing from Piccadilly Square to Paddington Station. Understanding the culture and knowing the destination beforehand can really pay off big time. When you know where you are going and what to look for, you're less likely to miss the treasures. For instance . . .

While visiting the quaint little town of Bath, I left everyone else at the Roman ruins to pay homage to Jane Austen with a quick tour of her home. After discovering its location in my guidebook, I made a beeline. Seriously, as if I could spend a summer in England and not go to see Miss Jane!? Yeah, right! I have no regrets about bypassing the lecture on Roman aqueducts. When there is a life-size replica of Mr. Darcy when you walk through the front door! Well, to be precise, it's a cutout of Colin Firth playing the character of Mr. Darcy, but that's just as good, right? (Disclaimer: If you don't know who Mr. Darcy is, I consider that a deal breaker in our friendship. Not to worry, you can rent or read *Pride and Prejudice*, understand my obsession, and fall in love with him for yourself. . . . Then our friendship will be back on track.) Yes, of course I took my picture with him; I mean *it!* Whatever. It's framed and in my bedroom. I'm obsessed. I know. Don't judge. Back to my point—my trip was so much more amazing because I took the time to learn a little bit about my destination.

With that in mind, this guidebook, designed to help women navigate our female friendships, should logically begin by clarifying what "friendship" is and what it is not. After all, we must know what we are looking for, or we will never experience God's best in these relationships. Trust me, we don't want to miss a thing!

What? You Too?

A man of many companions may come to ruin, but there is a friend who sticks closer than a brother. (Prov. 18:24 NIV)

One of the most famous statements defining friendship is from C. S. Lewis's book *The Four Loves.* Lewis, one of Christianity's most brilliant minds and greatest theologians, was known for his incredible lifelong friendship with a group called The Inklings. They shared a passion for life, literature, and Jesus. Gleaning from his own experience, Lewis writes:

> Friendship arises out of mere companionship when two or more of the companions discover that they have in common some insight or interest or even taste which the others do not share and which, till that moment, each believed to be his own unique treasure or burden. The typical expression of open-ing friendship would be something like, "What? You too? I thought I was the only one."[1]

Essentially Lewis says that friendship is birthed out of connection. Something unique draws us to a person and bonds us to her. His statement, "What? You too?" proves the perfect expression of how it feels when we meet someone and know that we've discovered a new friend.

I'll never forget the day that my friend Stephanie transformed from an acquaintance into one of my best friends. I was in the midst of a full-blown meltdown of mythic proportions when God brought her into my life. I was walking through a dark time after a heartbreak that tested my faith. The hardest part of that wilderness season was feeling so alone and thinking no one understood my pain. Most of my other close friends were married and starting motherhood, and they didn't get my struggle with singleness or the searing pain of rejection. Then one day Stephanie stopped by my house armed with Coke, cookies, and chick flicks. While I knew her socially, we weren't super-close friends at this point . . . although our status was about to change.

Stephanie sat down on my couch, handed me the breakup survival kit, and said, "I want to tell you my story." In her gentle and compassionate manner, she proceeded to open up and tell me about her own wilderness experience. She said, "A few years ago I was engaged to the man of my dreams. It was a fairy tale. I loved him. He loved me. Then we went home to visit my parents for Christmas, and on Christmas night he dropped the bomb. He broke our engagement." She really didn't have to say much more. I just knew. She got me.

"What? You too? I thought I was the only one."

Here's the beautiful thing about a good friendship—one can begin when you least expect it. Stephanie and I have remained close friends from that day forward, and I can pinpoint the exact moment we truly connected on a deep level to that moment when we bonded over our shared pain.

Heartbreak is not the only glue that bonds two girlfriends together. The bond can be a shared passion for running that grows into a lifelong friendship, or the connection can begin as simply as two women who meet because their kids are the same age and their relationship blossoms over the trials and tribulations of motherhood. Anything can spark a friendship, but not anyone can be a friend. So the question remains, what is a friend?

I like this definition: *a trustworthy peer with whom we choose to lovingly live in a relationship with unique access and service.*[2] This definition is a great starting point for our journey because it sets the parameters and scope of the relationships we will address in this book. This helps me because I am a woman who is incredibly social by nature and such an open book that I tend to call every woman I've ever met my friend. I'm not saying friendliness is wrong, but my purpose is to focus on the core relationships this guidebook will examine.

While women can hold many relationship titles— sister, spouse, daughter, mother, aunt, mentor, or boss— the relationship I focus on in this book is our female friendships. These are the women we *choose* to do life with, and they are not beholden to us as family members or coworkers. The nature of friendship is that it is optional. The choice to walk away is always there in a friendship, bringing with it a different set of

> *The* choice to walk away is always there in a friendship, bringing with it a different set of complexities and questions.

complexities and questions. Let's really break down this definition. First, a friend is a "trustworthy peer." She knows your stuff. She's got your back. She knows you have your lip waxed . . . but she's not tellin'. It's in the vault.

Second, this definition says a friend is someone who has "unique access." This is important to note because in our culture we use the term *friend* so loosely. I dare say that if most of the people we know on Facebook were to walk into our homes without notice, we'd be a little freaked out. But when your best friend stops by, she has "access." After all, she knows where you hide the spare key. She has access not only to your home but to your heart.

I call this the "refrigerator test." I know who my closest friends are by the comfort level we feel in each other's homes. With my best friends I will just open up their refrigerator and dig through it until I find the Diet Coke. I will help myself to last night's leftovers without thinking to ask for permission. With close friendships there's no pretense. Likewise, I know a friend feels close to me when she will do the same in my house. There's just so much symbolism tied up in this act of openness. Those are the types of friendships we will dive into and explore together, the ones that get close enough to our hearts to hurt us and to heal us.

Honestly, this type of relational access is precisely *why* we need a guidebook. When we get close to each other, life gets messy. Complications arise when our fears, insecurities, and struggles surface. A woman can find herself lost in a dark maze of pain and dysfunction and sin, not knowing how she got there or where to turn. Thankfully God's Word proves to be the light even in these dark places.

Third, as we dig into Scripture, we will see that the last part of our definition is key: a friend "serves." So often in our "what's in it for me?" culture, relationships are selfish. This is not friendship. A real friendship, as God defines one, is a relationship where each party seeks the best for the other and places the other's needs before her own.

This next statement may be a hard pill to swallow. Someone isn't really a friend if she is only in it for what *she* can get out of the relationship: power, popularity, prestige, or position. When someone is "working you," she's not your friend.

A friend is the girl who is there *for* you, expecting nothing for herself in return.

- A friend is there on moving day.
- A friend helps wash the dishes long after the dinner party is over and the guests have all cleared out.
- A friend listens to the breakup story again . . . and again . . . and again.
- A friend will patiently analyze and interpret the nuances of his text message . . . looking for hidden declarations of love.

- A friend senses a full-blown mommy meltdown and takes the kids for the afternoon.
- A friend sits in the doctor's office to hold your hand and hear the report.

True friends *serve* one another. Frankly, the person who isn't there in a time of need, who doesn't listen, who doesn't go the extra mile, isn't really a friend. She may be a wonderful social acquaintance, an esteemed coworker, a teammate, someone you respect in your mommy playgroup, or even a sorority sister, but she isn't a friend. Let's reclaim this word and make it special again. A friend is "a trustworthy peer with whom we choose to lovingly live in a relationship with unique access and service."

Can I hear an amen?

The Master of Ceremonies

Every good and perfect gift is from above, coming down from the Father of the heavenly lights. (James 1:17 NIV)

Now that we've defined *friendship*, let's consider *why* God gave us this gift. After all, He certainly didn't have to. Yet in His infinite goodness He did. God hardwired us for friendship. He placed in our hearts the desire for these relationships and the ability to form them. More important, in His wonderful sovereignty, the Lord orchestrates and weaves life's intersections together so that two individuals will cross paths and from that point forward walk together as friends. C. S. Lewis observed this truth by saying:

> We think we have chosen our peers. In reality, a few years' difference in the dates of our births, a few more miles between certain houses, the choice of one university instead of another, posting to different regiments, the accident of a topic being raised or not raised at a first meeting—any of these chances might have kept us apart. But, for a Christian, there are, strictly speaking, no chances. A secret Master of Ceremonies has been at work. Christ, who said to the disciples, "Ye have not chosen me, but I have chosen you," can truly say to every group of Christian friends, "You have not chosen one another but I have chosen you for one another. (Friendship) is His instrument for creating as well as revealing.[3]

Recalling the various moments God used to introduce me to the women who are my closest friends, I am awed by His handiwork. He actually has employed everything from boy crushes to Bible study classes, shared cubicles, and a shared love for Mexican food. He knew that I would need each one of these amazing women in my life in order to fulfill His purpose, and vice versa.

I have come to realize that friendships are not accidental or coincidental. God is extremely purposeful in all He does and wastes absolutely nothing. He has a purpose for our friendships. He places people in our path for seasons and reasons only fully known in His all-knowing and all-loving nature. Lewis perfectly describes this involvement (as quoted above) by comparing God to a secret Master of Ceremonies at work who chooses us for one another. This begs the question, *But why?*

What great purpose does God accomplish through friendships? I see three primary reasons in Scripture: first, companionship; next sanctification; and finally, so that we would serve one another.

Companionship

> The LORD God said, "It is not good for the man to be alone." (Gen. 2:18)

OK, so we typically understand this verse to be about the need for the helpmate God created for Adam, and that's definitely the context for this verse, but I think there is a broader reality to this statement and throughout Scripture. God wired us for relationships. In short, I so appreciate the fact that in one of the opening verses of Scripture God declares that it is not good for us to be alone.

Amen! Hallelujah. Thank you, Lord!

This truth causes a people person like me to let out a huge sigh of relief . . . and a few amens. In case you haven't picked up on this nugget of truth just yet, I don't like flying solo. For instance, even if I'm driving just a half a mile and I have the option of having a friend in the car or going the distance alone, of course I want my buddy with me! Or I've even heard crazy talk that some people *actually* go to the movies *alone*! What in the world? That takes all the fun out of the movies for me. I'm not judging, but if you are all alone, who in the world do you share your Twizzlers with? Or who is there to hear when you lean over and make really funny comments? Trust me, perfect strangers think you're just weird when you regale them with clever banter. I ask you ladies . . . nay, I challenge you to consider: Where in the world would we be without the companionship of girlfriends? I tell you exactly where we'd be—we'd be sitting alone in the movies wearing jeans that look horrible on us because no one was there in the dressing room to tell us that skinny-legged jeans are best left to Heidi Klum.

Life would simply be horrific without girlfriends.

Thankfully God is so good to us. He gives us sidekicks, copilots, dressing room critics, boy-crush analyzers, truth speakers, exercise buddies, and the "first call" friend when you fall in love or find yourself tragically heartbroken. We share life with our companions. This gift proves increasingly valuable as our culture delays marriage and as we live farther and farther away from our parents and siblings. In this day and age friends are like family.

Companionship is golden. As Les Parrott so aptly said, "The world is a wilderness without good friends."[4] God knows us, after all, He formed us in our mother's wombs. He understands that we need community and He created us as such. We aren't good alone; we need the fellowship of friendship.

Loneliness cripples the human spirit. A good friend alleviates this condition. One of the simplest and sweetest blessings of fellowship is the sheer presence of another person. I think we take good companionship for granted until faced with a season of solitude or loneliness.

I'll never forget watching the movie *Castaway*, starring Tom Hanks. In this film Hanks portrays a man whose plane crashes, leaving him washed ashore on a remote island. While his physical survival is crucial, his mental survival is at risk as well, due to his sheer isolation and loneliness. For sanity he creates a friend. Wilson is his name—a volleyball marked with eyes, a nose, and a mouth, that becomes his only companion. The saddest moment in the film is when Wilson floats away when the two are floating at sea awaiting rescue. The guttural cry of pain that comes forth from Tom Hanks is heartbreaking. Echoing through my mind as I watched his plight was . . .

"It is not good for the man to be alone."

Sanctification

For this is God's will, your sanctification. (1 Thess. 4:3)

Anytime I see the words in Scripture, "This is God's will," I sit up and take notice, grab my highlighter, underline the words in red, and write them on a sticky note. This verse is straightforward and clearly spells out that God's will for my life and for your life is *sanctification*. Technically this term means "to make holy." He desires that you and I reflect His holiness to the world.

Simply stated, sanctification is transformation. It is the process whereby we are being transformed from our old sinful nature to become more and more like Jesus. Let me stress that this is a lifelong process. True transformation of anything does not happen overnight. In our world of extreme makeovers, we are bent toward wanting and believing in instant reformation, redecoration, reconstruction, and refashionizing! However, when the camera lenses are capped, the lighting is unplugged, and the limitless budget of the produced results are gone, has there really been a true transformation, or are we left with a counterfeit?

Authentic transformation occurs under God's tender hand: a winter-barren tree bursting forth in new green shoots; an awkward scraggly gosling maturing into a regal, snow-white swan; a stumpy, bumpy caterpillar sprouting gossamer wings and flying high and free. And so it is with our sanctification. Under God's tender hand we undergo a metamorphosis . . . one that sets us on a more beautiful and more freeing course. From the moment we accept Christ as Savior, our transformation begins. The Bible describes this beginning as our "new birth." Just as a newborn caterpillar grows stronger as it struggles against the cocoon until it breaks free as a new creation, we, too, struggle against insecurities, hurt feelings, misunderstandings, rejections, and disappointments until we overcome the old sinful nature and experience the freedom of life in Christ.

You might be asking yourself, "What does all this have to do with friendship?" I'm so glad you asked! One of God's primary transformation tools is the refining process of relationships. In a relationship—romantic, family, or friendships— our junk is exposed. We see our selfishness. We see our pride. And when these areas are revealed, if we choose to turn from our sin, receive God's grace and the empowerment of His Spirit, then we are transformed, becoming more like Jesus.

> **God's primary transformation tool is the refining process of relationships. In a relationship—romantic, family, or friendships—our junk is exposed.**

In friendship, especially among close friends, we get real. We see the good, the bad, and the ugly. Issues and conflicts arise, exposing our capacity for good as well as evil. We call it our "baggage." Open it up and you'll find unbelief, unhealed wounds, unforgiveness, and unconfessed sin. We will delve into the specifics of transformation in future chapters, but for now realize this: One of God's primary purposes for friendships is to reveal our baggage to us, to mature us, so that we will reflect Jesus more and more to the world. Ultimately, as we are sanctified, we will love as Jesus loves, speak as Jesus speaks, and befriend as Jesus befriends.

The Hands and Feet of Christ

> A friend loves at all times, and a brother is born for adversity. (Prov. 17:17 NIV)

I find myself searching for the exact word to describe a rather unpleasant situation that I had to endure a while back. Awkward doesn't even come close to cutting it. Horrific. Dreadful. Searing. Painful. Nauseating. . . . OK, so you get the picture. Truly, I've never dreaded a moment as much as I did this impending meeting that required both confrontation and forgiveness on my part.

As any girl in my shoes would do, I picked up the phone and called one of my best friends, Tonya, to download the drama of my impending anguish. Choking back tears, I felt painful memories sweep over me while everything in me screamed, "Don't make me do this!" Of course, Tonya listened with compassion—she always listens. She prayed with me as I drove my car toward the meeting spot; she always prays, but little did I know the rest of the story.

Facing the situation head-on, I arrived at the restaurant for the dreaded encounter. As the minutes ticked by in this difficult meeting, something strange began to occur. I sensed the horribleness—yes, I said horribleness—of it all lifting. My dread (and queasiness) was actually being replaced by a new sensation: God's presence and peace began to surround me and fill me with unexplainable joy. Joy! The remedy to my situation was a mystery. That is, it was mystery until I walked back out to my car and discovered a note on my windshield. It read:

Marian,

I couldn't stand the thought of you facing this alone. After we hung up the phone, I drove over here and I've been sitting out here in my car praying for you the entire time. I could see you through the window while I prayed. I love you. Jesus loves you more than you can imagine. I'm proud of you for facing this.

—Tonya

You have no idea how loved I felt in that moment. Truly, I felt as if Jesus Himself met me there and stood guard in my time of need. I wasn't alone. In a tangible way God was with me using my friend to be His hands and feet. Yes, on that bleak, cold, winter day, my sweet friend sat in her car, motor running, heat blaring, and prayers availing! That moment stands out in my mind as the perfect example of God's intention for friendship—that we would be instruments of hope and healing and comfort and care to those the Master of Ceremonies places in our path.

No love of the natural heart is safe unless the human heart has been satisfied by God first.

—Oswald Chambers

The Perfect Travel Companion

Screeching brakes broke the quiet morning calm. The alarming noise was quickly followed by a whirlwind of chaos as our luggage catapulted through the air with the ease of an Olympic gymnast. Coffee cups and croissants joined the fun by doing somersaults into our laps—scoring a perfect ten for the dismount. Dodging a flying duffle bag, I looked up at my friend Keri, as we tumbled to the ground, and said, "This is sooooooo not normal!"

TRAVEL ADVISORY: THERE'S ABSOLUTELY NOTHING NORMAL ABOUT A TRAIN WRECK IN EASTERN EUROPE.

Crisscrossing Europe by rail is hands down the best way to experience the continent. What American can resist the enchantment of hopping on a train in Rome, falling asleep, only to awaken in Paris by morning? I've taken advantage of this incredible rail system on each of my European adventures—London to Paris, Berlin to

Munich, Florence to Pisa, and everything in between; but no amount of experience prepared me for a full-blown train wreck.

My friend Keri and I were at the tail end of a three-week tour when we found ourselves sitting on the tracks somewhere in Eastern Europe. I kicked off the journey in Germany as part of a mission trip to Berlin. I met up with Keri in Munich, and from there we set out to visit the countries of Austria, Hungary, Czech Republic, and France. After twirling and singing like Maria from *The Sound of Music* on the Austrian mountainside (yes, indeed, the hills are still alive with the sound of it), we commenced to eat our weight in Sacher torte (by far the best chocolate cake that'll ever cross your lips) in Vienna before exploring the magnificent Budapest.

I'd been to Europe a few times before, but this was Keri's first adventure. So, with all of my "European experience," I assumed the role of tour guide and sage advisor to my friend, the novice. Therefore, from time to time, Keri likes to point out in retelling our escapade that I would assure her with the phrase, *"This is normal."*

"When we cross the border between Germany and Austria, be prepared, they will ask for your passport. This is normal."

"Our french fries in France will actually come with mayonnaise instead of ketchup. This is normal!"

"There will be no ice in your Pepsi. This is normal."

"Eastern Europeans consider wool a fine summer wardrobe choice. This is normal."

And indeed, everything was "normal" when we caught the early morning train to Prague. We had high expectations for a destination brimming with both history and culture. I'd read so much about this city that I couldn't wait to see it firsthand. Our expectations for our transportation were somewhat lower. Trust me, the minute we walked into the station, we knew we weren't dealing with fabulous Eurostar luxury anymore (high-speed bullet trains with modern amenities). Nope, our train appeared to be a relic from the World War II era. Seriously, a horse and buggy would have been just as high tech. Now that I think about it, our expectations should have been lower.

Once settled in our compartment, we placed our coffee and croissants on the table separating us. Keri grabbed her book, while I rested my head against the window, watching the countryside roll along. Lulled to sleep by the rhythmic click clacking of the old train, I was jolted awake when I felt the initial thump of wheels skidding off rail. Objects didn't stop flying until we finally capsized onto the gravel edge. *Not normal! Not normal! Not normal!*

With adrenaline pumping and eyes bulging, we stared at each other. Once we processed what had just happened and realized that we were totally fine and injury free, we laughed until our sides ached. *A train wreck . . . seriously? Did that just happen? This is too good. Should we even bother to call our mothers?*

Finding our strewn bags, we joined the other passengers sitting outside on the tracks. Looking around after the dust cleared, I noticed all sorts of reactions ranging from hysteria to humor. Some people dealt with the stressful situation with anger while others just waited patiently for the "rescue" train to pick us up. We took the opportunity to have an impromptu photo shoot on the train tracks. After all, we'd need plenty of evidence back in the USA (and of course, the tale would grow larger and larger with each telling).

Today, in this retelling, I'm incredibly thankful that I had Keri by my side. She's a great travel companion—spontaneous yet organized, laid-back yet assertive when needed, able to laugh at trials yet filled with compassion. But even more, she's a great friend. Remembering that moment on the tracks, I can't help but think of how similar that scene is to this journey we call life. There are times when it feels like everything goes off track, and your heart is skidding into the gravel. During those scary moments the luggage flying in your face may land scarred among the rocky terrain of sickness, infertility, heartbreak, rejection, financial crisis, or fear. It really doesn't matter the situation. It's always a relief to know you have a good friend by your side when you're stuck waiting on the tracks for the rescue.

This is one of God's greatest blessings in friendship: the companionship that only a good friend can provide. Honestly, none of us ever really knows when life is going to derail and you find yourself sitting by the road in need of rescue. One of God's supreme gifts in these seasons is the provision of friends. Thankfully we don't have to sit alone. When you have a good friend, a faithful companion, you have someone with you on those tracks who says, "OK, this is not normal. But you are not alone." While there are untold blessings found in a great friendship, there is a surefire way to train wreck one.

How to Train Wreck a Good Friendship—Make It an Idol!

In girl world, a best friend represents security. Someone to always shop/hang out/lay out with. What girl doesn't want a sense of security? —Kim, age 20

What girl doesn't want a best friend? A loyal companion who is always there for her, who understands her completely, and who listens attentively. The longing for this person runs deep in our souls. I've seen this desire played out in little girls and grown women alike. Young girls want someone to share the coveted best-friend necklace, secret crushes, and the lunch table in the cafeteria. Grown women crave the same thing, although we've exchanged the necklace for titles such as "maid of honor" or "my bestie," and we've traded in the cafeteria lunch table for a standing Saturday brunch date.

The television show *Grey's Anatomy* depicts this type of close friendship between characters Meredith Grey and

Cristina Yang. Describing each other as their "person" signifies their status. They see each other through "dark and twisty" and "bright and shiny" times; they see the real, the raw, and the ugly. This code name for best friend implies that they are each other's first call in an emergency, and their relationship is given preeminence over others.

While it's true that close companionship is a gift from God, even the best of friendships can become dysfunctional if unrealistic expectations are placed upon the relationship. There is a point when our legitimate need for companionship can take an unhealthy turn and result in its own kind of train wreck. God intends our relationships and the order of our relationships to follow a priority He has given us. Look at what He says in Colossians 1:18, talking about Jesus: "He is also the head of the body, the church; He is the beginning, the firstborn from the dead, so that He might come to have first place in everything." Jesus is supposed to be first.

The best of friendships can become dysfunctional if unrealistic expectations are placed upon the relationship.

If the cry of our hearts for love and acceptance is not first realized in a relationship with Jesus Christ, then great disappointment awaits any woman who believes she'll find it in a friendship. The bottom line is this: Our best girl friend, on her best day, with the best of intentions, cannot make us feel secure if we are not already secure because of our position in Christ.

Throughout life, I've felt insecure with acceptance from other girls, whether or not a girl liked me enough to consider me a friend or regarded me as more fun to hang around than another. I grew up with a brother and in a neighborhood of all boys. I didn't really know how to relate to girls that well. Therefore, I didn't know what to talk to them about and always feared them judging me for not being up to par with them in how a girl should be. I notice these thoughts spring to mind when I take my focus away from the cross . . . because if I kept my eyes on Christ the whole time, I would not need to find acceptance in the opinions of girls, but I would always know that I am accepted by the most beloved King. —Presley, age 32

Whatever our age or stage in the game, the issue at hand is one of belonging. Since as women we derive much of our identity from relationships, it makes sense that we would draw a great deal of significance and security from our friendships. We long to feel special, valued. We want to know that someone has our back and will always be there in our time of need.

In Robert McGee's pivotal book, *The Search for Significance*, he uses the term "emotional dependency" to describe relational idolatry. He writes, "Emotional dependency is the condition resulting when the ongoing presence and/or nurturing of another is believed necessary for personal security."[1]

With the dual desires for significance and security comes a cargo load of fears, unmet expectations, and disappointments—the natural consequences of attempting to draw significance and security from another person. Let's face it, no human being can meet our needs 100 percent of the time or answer the cry in our hearts about our worth and value. And if we are completely honest with ourselves, we know that we certainly can't meet those longings in others.

I feel like we hold them (best friends) up on a pedestal, but then we are devastated when we realize that they are human like us and fall short. For instance, we get so frustrated when a friend says the wrong thing to us or hurts our feelings in some way. Also, the more you hang out with someone, the more you get to know all of them, including faults. This can cause disappointment because we held them in higher regards, but we must realize that our friends are sinners too who are trying to turn from their wounded ways like us. —Katie, age 26

When a woman relies on her status or standing for confidence and security in a friendship, she misplaces her significance. This lethal cocktail will kill even the best of friendships and generate fear—

- Fear of losing status in a friendship can result in jealousy if one suspects her friend of growing closer to another.
- Fear of rejection leads many women to conform or perform to maintain relationship status.
- Fear can also lead to possessiveness or manipulation if one feels her standing in the friendship is threatened.

The reason relational fears reside in our hearts will be addressed specifically when we examine our baggage in upcoming chapters, but before we get into the nitty-gritty of these issues, we can and must deal with the greatest problem affecting friendship: the fact that no one can be our source of security and significance other than Jesus Christ. To give anyone that power is to make her a god. Idolatry.

Yep, you heard me right.

When you and I hand over the power to make ourselves feel secure to another person, we make an idol of that person. This is called "relational idolatry," and this is a huge red flag in friendship. Author Dee Brestin commented on this perversion in her book *The Friendships of Women*, "As women, our tendency toward dependency on people is our Achilles' heel. We engage in 'relational idolatry' with both friends and husbands, forgetting that our real security is in God."[2] *Relational idolatry*? Yes, that is a strong term but a needed one. We need to recognize that friendships characterized by guilt, fear, manipulation, exhausting demands, and a general lack of freedom are so "not normal"!

Relational idolatry will destroy and divide even the best of friends. Yes, I said destroy. The reason is simple. A relationship cannot stand that kind of pressure. Projecting our need for belonging in a friendship places a burden on the relationship that will ultimately cause it to crumble under the strain of unmet expectations and insecurities. As I recently told a group of young women in a Bible study class, "No one can be your Jesus, except Jesus."

Only One saves us.

Only One defines us.

Only One completes us.

Only One truly lays down His life for us.

If we look to a friend to meet our emotional needs, we will be highly disappointed. No one can rightfully sit on the throne of the human heart other than Jesus Christ. Attempting to put another in His place leads only to disappointment, which causes its own downward spiral: Disappointment results in hurt feelings, bitterness, anger, and all sorts of defensive reactions. Can anyone say "drama"?

> *P*rojecting our need for belonging . . . places a burden on the relationship that will ultimately cause it to crumble under the strain of unmet expectations and insecurities.

Yikes! So, what's a girl to do? Here are three practical steps:

1. Recognize the Problem

We must own up to the problem and recognize relational idolatry as sin. Idolatry in any form is the exaltation of something or someone to a higher place than God Himself. The first two of the Ten Commandments address the issue of idolatry head on:

> And God spoke all these words: "I am the LORD your God, who brought you out of Egypt, out of the land of slavery. You shall have no other gods before me. You shall not make for yourself an idol in the form of anything in heaven above or on the earth beneath or in the waters below. You shall not bow down to them or worship them; for I, the LORD your God, am a jealous God." (Exod. 20:1–5 NIV)

Our modern culture often thinks of idols as small wooden objects worshipped in other religions. In reality, anything can serve as an idol—people, possessions, money, status, and even a friendship. Yet God is clear. Our hearts are not safe until they are fully His. Our tendency toward idolatry plagues the human race. Yet God loves us so much that He won't allow any idol to stand in His rightful place. If we put a relationship at a higher place in our hearts, He will tear it down. Trust me.

The One worthy of our hearts is the Lord.

The source of our significance is the Lord.

Our security is the Lord.

The One who defines us is the Lord.

He is a jealous God. Jealous *for* us. Since idolatry destroys anything it touches, especially relationships, God commands us to remove idols from our hearts. Does this mean the friendship must end? No! But we must first recognize if we are exalting the friendship to a place that isn't godly.

Here's how: Ask yourself these tough questions.

- Are my expectations of my friend concerning time, communication, and availability realistic?
- Is my friend expecting too much of me?
- Do I frequently, unintentionally hurt her?
- Do I feel totally free and myself with this person?
- Do I walk on eggshells in order to please?
- Do I feel possessive or threatened?
- Do I obsess in fear about losing the friend?
- Is my identity tied to the friendship? Status, ranking, popularity?
- Do I have a history of failed close friendships? Why?
- Have I conformed myself or my values to meet a friend's demands or in order to fit into a group?
- Am I drawing an inappropriate amount of security from this relationship?

While this list isn't exhaustive, it does give us an idea of subtle ways relational idolatry can materialize in a friendship. In order for our relationships to glorify God, we must ask ourselves these tough questions and recognize when we've placed too much weight on a friendship—a weight that only Jesus is truly able to bear.

Friendships are unhealthy when relational idolatry is allowed to stand. We must remember that a healthy, God-honoring friendship is one where two people are turned outward (drawing security from God) rather than inward (attempting to draw security from one another). In *The Four Loves* by C. S. Lewis, he describes the proper stance of a healthy friendship: "Lovers are always talking to one another about their love; friends hardly ever talk about their friendship. Lovers are normally face to face, absorbed in each other; friends, side by side, absorbed in some common interest."[3]

If or when a friendship is emotionally dependent or unhealthy, there will always be a lack of freedom. "Healthy relationships encourage individuality rather than conformity and are concerned with independence rather than emotional dependence. Healthy relationships point one's focus to the Lord and pleasing Him rather than toward the friendship and pleasing one another."[4] Ask God today to help you recognize any areas of relational idolatry or emotional dependence and to turn you or your friend's heart back to Him.

2. Repent

Here's a completely and utterly embarrassing confession: Relational idolatry was once a huge struggle in my life. From the time I was a young girl until I was a grown woman out of college, I placed my hope for security and desire for significance in the relationships in my life. This problem manifested in compromising my values in order to maintain certain friendships, pushing away friends with my high expectations, draining relationships with constant need for security, and battling feelings of jealousy over other relationships.

What would cause me to react this way? The answer is twofold. First, I had some serious baggage that needed to be addressed. But also, I was not looking to my relationship with Jesus Christ to meet my emotional needs, nor was I trusting Him for acceptance and approval. Instead I attempted in vain to draw my legitimate needs from illegitimate sources.

I learned the hard way that there's only one Jesus. I can write this book because I've been there. Guilty as charged. It took the ending of several key friendships for me to see clearly that my fears, hurts, unmet expectations, and relational struggles were rooted in a heart hungry for the belonging that can only be found in a relationship with God.

Before we gloss over this issue or falsely assume, let me clarify something quickly: Relational idolatry is not just an issue for women who don't know Jesus. Christians and non-Christians alike can struggle with this issue. Trust me, at the time in life when I realized my sin, I knew Jesus! In fact, I loved Jesus, and I trusted Jesus! Yet I was still looking to relationships to fill a void in my life that only God can fill.

After several train-wreck friendships, I finally identified my unhealthy pattern and turned to God for help. Recognizing my sin, I repented of relational idolatry and fully turned to Christ. Listen closely friends: Repentance always means change. Recognition alone is not enough! Repentance evidences itself with a new way of living and relating. I can tell you one thing: by God's grace I have changed!

While not a popular word these days, repentance is the only solution to idolatry. How this works in the realm of relational idolatry is that we turn from placing our hope for significance and security in a person and place it fully in Christ. While relational idolatry can be a two-way street, the only person I can change is myself. The only person you can change is yourself. We must choose to turn away from this sin and allow God to handle our friend's sin in His own way and time.

Repentance means that we surrender our friend and our unhealthy expectations of the friendship to God, asking Jesus' forgiveness for seeking security in someone other than Him. Are you curious what this looks like? Here's an example of a prayer that highlights repentance for this sin:

Jesus, I confess that (fill in the name) is a blessing from you as a friend, but I've looked to this person for security, identity, and significance. Forgive me for putting an unhealthy burden on this friendship. Please forgive me for relational idolatry. Jesus, I pray that You alone would reign in my heart and help me draw my legitimate need for belonging from You and You alone. I bless (fill in the name) and I release her to you. I pray You will heal any damage done to our friendship by my sin.

Today I recognize the temptation to draw my legitimate needs for security and significance from someone other than Jesus. So when I find myself struggling with hurt feelings or jealousy, I quickly assess *why*. It's always good to take a step back and evaluate emotions. If a legitimate wrong has been done to me, then I have the choice to forgive and address the issue with my friend. However, if the hurt is derived from an unmet expectation or fear of losing my place of importance in a friendship, then I know that I need to repent and release the person to God.

3. Reconnect with God's Truth

For change to be real and lasting, God's truth must replace the lies we believe. Typically, when it comes to relational idolatry, the lies are usually associated with where we find our value, significance, identity, security, and acceptance (belonging). Satan will always tempt us to find this anywhere other than our relationship with God. The enemy loves it when we turn from facing God, deriving our security from Him, to facing man and vainly hoping to feel loved and accepted by another mere mortal's approval, while exhausting ourselves in the process. Satan targets this legitimate need for belonging by tempting us to think we can attain our heart's desire by grasping onto a human relationship (a best friend).

We clamor to feel important.

We fight to secure our spot in the friendship.

We continually strive to feel approved.

As I've said, repentance means turning away from the idol (a person) and turning back to God. This is only the first step. Next we dismantle the lies that got us in the mess in the first place. To walk in relational freedom, we must reconnect with God's truth until the lies we've believed are destroyed.

Here's the truth: From the beginning God has desired a personal relationship with us where we are one with Him and derive our sense of belonging, security, significance, and confidence from His love. This is our original design. Consequently, when the relationship between man and God was broken, all other human relationships went down hill as a result (Gen. 3). Therefore, not only are we in need of redemption from sin, but we also need freedom from the lies we've believed while its prisoner. Thankfully Jesus said,

"You will know the truth, and the truth will set you free" (John 8:32).

The key to wholeness and freedom in all of our relationships is found in placing supreme priority on our relationship with Christ and by allowing His truth to penetrate deep in our hearts and transform how we see others and ourselves.

Oh, how He loves us!

The night before His crucifixion, Jesus said, "No one has greater love than this, that someone would lay down his life for his friends" (John 15:13). Jesus alone is the perfect friend—He demonstrated His love for us and says with arms stretched out on the cross, "You are worth dying for!" In relationship with Him, we look to Him first to seek our approval from His words, and not only does He tell us that we are fully accepted, but He says far more than that, "I will never leave you or forsake you" (Heb. 13:5).

Oh, what a friend we have in Jesus!

Christ Jesus, the Perfect Friend

Beholding the love of God poured out to us in Jesus is like staring into the sun at full strength. The brightness eclipses all the dark doubts and insecurities that tempt us to turn to another to feel loved and accepted. Friends, it is imperative that we daily look to Jesus. Turn to the One who is the perfect friend and allow Him to meet your needs for love and acceptance. There's a beautiful bonus to God's love: it casts out all fear. As Scripture says, "God is love.

Whoever lives in love lives in God, and God in him. In this way, love is made complete among us so that we will have confidence . . . There is no fear in love. But perfect love drives out fear" (1 John 4:16–18 NIV).

God's perfect love dismantles the lie of relational idolatry. Resting in His perfect acceptance, unconditional belonging, and unwavering loyalty rids the human heart of the fears that cripple and kill relationships. As Dan Allender perfectly explains, "Christ's death not only creates a relationship with God, but also allows us to have meaningful relationships with other people."[5] As our guide in navigating female friendships, Jesus begins the journey by calling us back to Himself. When He is our best friend and we find our belonging in Him, then and only then can we experience friendship as He intended.

If you are anything like me, I'm sure you've struggled with this issue from time to time. What our hearts need is to draw life and security from the One who will never fail, Jesus Christ. Some of you may be thinking, "That sounds great, Marian, but how in the world do I know Jesus as my best friend?" Deepening your friendship with God happens the same way you would grow any other friendship; two essential ingredients are required: communication and time!

Make Jesus Your BFF

To avoid the train wreck of relational idolatry, each of us must choose to make Jesus our BFF. Deepening this relationship starts with authentic communication.

Girls, you know nothing bonds us together like talking. The same holds true for our friendship with God. Determine to spend time with Jesus on a daily basis. Make time with Him the priority of your day. In these times He speaks to us through His Word, and we speak to Him in prayer. Then, throughout your day, turn to Him with your struggles and fears and open up your heart to Him as you would a friend. The Bible calls this "praying without ceasing." It's like having Jesus on speed dial. He's at the top of your top friend list and your first call in time of need. The problem is that we are more likely to seek out a person in these situations rather than God. Too often we run to the phone before we run to the throne.

Oh, friends, we must turn to Jesus! When God is at the center of our hearts, when we turn to Him first for belonging, then and only then will we have the type of friendship we need and desire.

Putting God first in our lives helps us to see that we have only one certain relationship in which the other loves us unconditionally. Jesus Christ knows our ugly side, and he loves us anyway. Instead of recoiling from us, he moves more passionately into our lives. If we open our hearts to both his unfailing love and the certain failure of all other love, then we will no longer be surprised by betrayal, but will anticipate how it can deepen our love for Christ. . . . Our relationship with Christ is the footing that makes all other relationships not only possible, but even potentially rich.[6]

Ironically, when a woman finds her significance from Jesus and His words, wholeness and freedom in human relationships become possible.

I've also discovered an incredible truth: a woman who is secure in Christ, confident in His love, and filled by His life, will draw other women to herself. There's something magnetic about freedom. Likewise, people naturally withdraw from a woman who sucks them dry with her neediness. But a woman whose cup is full of God's love will never feel short of friends because His love pours into her and out of her. So, it seems, in putting God back in His rightful place, we, in turn, get our heart's desire for friendship. Wow, isn't God smart?

➡ Girlfriend Guidebook Tip ⬅

Don't train wreck a friendship with relational idolatry. Surrender each relationship to Jesus and ask Him to be your number-one source of security and confidence.

What a friend we have in Jesus,
All our sins and griefs to bear!
What a privilege to carry
Everything to God in prayer!
Oh, what peace we often forfeit,
Oh, what needless pain we bear,
All because we do not carry
Everything to God in prayer!

Are we weak and heavy laden,
Cumbered with a load of care?
Precious Savior, still our refuge;
Take it to the Lord in prayer:
Do thy friends despise, forsake thee?
Take it to the Lord in prayer;
In His arms He'll take and shield thee;
Thou wilt find a solace there.

—Joseph Scriven, "What a Friend We Have in Jesus"

Deal with Your Baggage: Part I

Laying Down the Friendship Destroyers of Pride, Envy, and Competition

Remember when I mentioned earlier that I had backpacked Europe? Well, what I didn't mention was that it took some convincing by my girlfriends for me to agree to do so. Yes, it took some convincing. This not-so-granola girl strapped on a metal-frame backpack and acted like her own sherpa for two solid weeks. Here's a tip from one female traveler to another: *backpacks and high heels are not a great combo.*

The idea of backpacking Europe sounded so novel, so very "back to basics," so low maintenance of me. Back then I liked to think of myself as a "low maintenance" kind of girl. You know that really practical chick who can get by for two weeks on one pair of jeans, one pair of shoes, two T-shirts, and a few undies that she washes in the sink.

Trust me when I say that the mystique of roughing it wore off on day one.

I now own the fact that I am a high-maintenance traveler. I like my stuff: hair dryer, multiple shoe options, toiletries, daily wardrobe changes, and, yes, clean underwear. Plus, a girl's got to have space for all her purchases. After all, it's Europe! Seriously, how could I be expected to be in the land of leather (Italy) and not buy anything?

Today I've faced the facts: I'm a Texas girl with Texas hair, and nothing about me likes schlepping my stuff in and out of hostels and train stations across five countries. I'm self-aware. I embrace it: I'm not a low-maintenance traveler. Judge me if you'd like, but I prefer a nice, big, roller suitcase and preferably a doorman who'll carry it up to my room. Now that we have that straight, I can return to the story.

So my friends and I were rushing to check out of our hotel in Rome so that we could arrive at the train station on time for an overnight trip to Paris. By the time we managed to squeeze our two weeks' worth of necessities plus our week's worth of shopping back into our backpacks, we were a few minutes away from missing the train. Running out the door to catch the rest of the crew, my friend Jennifer and I bolted toward the elevator at the exact same moment. This is when our day got really interesting. Jennifer and I dove into the tiny European-sized elevator, barely fitting our arms and legs through, when a major problem developed. We couldn't close the elevator door. Between my seventy-pound backpack and hers, the elevator door was completely jammed against our packs. In such a confined space our backpacks formed a blockade that left us unable to budge. Wedged together, unable to move anything but our flailing arms, we realized that our backpacks had us pinned, which sent us into a bit of a frenzy as precious seconds ticked away on the clock.

Missing train!

Missing Paris!

Oh! No! I am so not missing Paris!

As the metal frame squeezed air from my lungs, visions of the Eiffel Tower flittered through my mind, and my penchant for a good fruit tart (a delicious and delicate pastry puff filled with sweet cream and topped with fresh fruit from some quaint little farm in France) roused my adrenaline into action. Determined and desperately craving sugar, I inhaled deeply, trying to squeeze out of the jam. Squirming proved pointless. My first instinct was to push, but the more we fought against each other, the worse our predicament became.

After "politely" yelling at each other to move, it became crystal clear that if we were going to get out of our predicament, we had to deal with our baggage. Our overweight and overstuffed packs were the cause of the conflict; therefore one of us needed to take off our backpack if we were going to get out of our mess. Since I wasn't about to miss Paris, I didn't hesitate slipping my shoulders out of the harness, crawling underneath my bag, and pulling it down onto the floor with me. Once I was free from my backpack, Jennifer was then able to turn around, scoot away from the door, and pull the elevator closed. Sweet freedom! Thankfully we caught the train and eventually made it to Paris, where we had an absolute blast. But it was nearly missed because of our stinkin' baggage!

I've seen this same type of predicament play out in female friendships. Feelings of frustration, resentment, and tension surface when two personalities rub up against each other—this is relational baggage. Just between us girls, if we are completely honest with ourselves, we know relational baggage can jam up a friendship just as my overweight backpack jammed up that Italian elevator.

> *F*eelings of frustration, resentment, and tension surface when two personalities rub up against each other—this is relational baggage.

While our baggage isn't of the physical nature, it can still take a toll on our friendships when we get close, causing hurt feelings, miscommunications, awkward silences, and uncomfortable encounters. Every girl must deal with two primary baggage issues when it comes to her female friendships. The first is our sinful nature, and the second, which we will discuss in the next chapter, is our unhealed wounds. If left unchecked, both can divide even the best of friends.

The Sinful Nature

OK, let's all just take a deep breath. Inhale deeply. Exhale slowly. I think it would be best if we tackle the biggest problem facing friendship first. (Yes, I'm a big fan of just ripping off the Band-Aid.) We all need to own something together: each of us has a sinful nature (Rom. 3:23). I know, I know, that's not a popular statement in this day and age, but it's the truth. In order to deal with our baggage effectively, we must face the fact that we have faults before we attempt to help others see theirs.

Each one of us is born sinful with our natures bent toward selfishness and rebellion against God. But here's the good news: when we accept Christ as Savior, we receive a new nature (2 Cor. 5:17). Now we have the Holy Spirit of God living within us. He (the Holy Spirit) enables us to live in a way that glorifies Jesus and leads us to keep God's commandments, which are all summed up in one statement: love God and love others (1 John 4:7–13).

Sounds pretty simple, huh?

Not so fast! Here's the major issue at hand. Even though as Christians we have a new nature (one that is holy, blameless, and redeemed), we still have our old sinful nature that we must deal with—this is our baggage. A follower of Jesus has a war going on inside; this war is the battle between our old sinful nature and the Holy Spirit who dwells within us. Paul explains this battle in this helpful passage from Galatians:

> The entire law is summed up in a single command: *"Love your neighbor as yourself."* If you keep on biting and devouring each other, watch out or you will be destroyed by each other.
>
> So I say, live by the Spirit, and you will not gratify the desires of the sinful nature. For *the sinful nature desires what is contrary to the Spirit,* and the Spirit what is contrary to the sinful nature. They are in conflict with each other, so that you do not do what you want. But if you are led by the Spirit, you are not under law.
>
> The acts of the sinful nature are obvious: sexual immorality, impurity and debauchery; idolatry and witchcraft; *hatred, discord, jealousy, fits of rage, selfish ambition, dissensions, factions and envy;* drunkenness, orgies, and the like. I warn you, as I did before, that those who live like this will not inherit the kingdom of God.
>
> But the fruit of the Spirit is love, joy, peace, patience, kindness, goodness, faithfulness, gentleness and self-control. Against such things there is no law. Those who belong to Christ Jesus have crucified the sinful nature with its passions and desires. Since we live by the Spirit, let us keep in

step with the Spirit. Let us not become conceited, provoking and envying each other. (Gal. 5:14–26 NIV, author emphasis)

I hope you noticed several key points in this passage. First, God calls us to love others by the power of His Spirit who lives within us. Second, and incredibly important to our discussion, there is a battle. Third, all of our human drama and conflict can be traced back to the sin nature that still resides in all of us. As Paul says, this sin nature is selfish and is the opposite of God's love. Finally, don't miss the most important point: as Christians, we have the potential to live by the power of our old sinful nature or by the power of the Holy Spirit. The question in every situation and temptation is this: Which one will we choose?

Since the sin nature is one of the biggest causes of relational drama, we need to understand fully how it wreaks havoc on our friendships. Our sin nature manifests itself in our relationships through the friendship destroyers of pride, envy, and competition. Let's look at each of these and how friendships are destroyed by them.

Pride

The Bible calls pride the root of all sin. Proverbs 13:10 says that it is "the root of all quarrels" (author paraphrase). ALL quarrels? Yep, all! This poisonous root springs up with weeds ripe for relational strife. Pride says, . . . *rather* it huffs . . .

- I am entitled to . . .
- I want to be first . . .
- I am right . . .
- I need to be the best . . .
- I deserve . . .
- I am not the one who needs to apologize . . .
- I have the right to . . .
- I want the credit . . .
- I want to be number one . . .
- I want to be noticed . . .
- I will be applauded . . .
- I need to be praised . . .
- I want my way . . .
- I need to be important . . .

Pride is not pretty. Pride destroys and divides and even leaves collateral damage in its wake. Pride focuses on self. This results in anger, hurt feelings, resentment, and bitterness; these emotions cause women to act defensively and put up walls. After all, it's tough to grow closer and develop a strong friendship when one or both persons in the relationship are thinking primarily about themselves.

Recently I met a girlfriend of mine to catch up over coffee. She asked about the manuscript for this book, and we talked at length about the baggage issues that affect female friendships. The issue of pride came up, and she said, "Oh, Marian, do I have the best illustration for you." My friend was once a cheerleading coach, and she witnessed how easily pride can cause women to turn against one another and divide those who were once best friends.

Every afternoon at cheerleading practice the girls would laugh and joke with one another as they stretched and prepared for the day. Throughout the year certain girls would click with each other, and it quickly became clear which ones were closest. Alliances formed and they were tight. Loyalty was huge, and girls often bragged about the closeness of their friendships. During practice they'd make weekend plans, share boyfriend stories, and swap outfits. From an outsider's perspective, their friendships seemed close, unshakable even. I'll never forget the day I saw how easily pride can divide a friendship.

As the cheer coach, I had to determine which stunts the squad would perform at pep rallies and place the girls in their spots. Here's the deal . . . every girl wanted to be on top, lifted high, and flying through the air during the basket toss. But the reality is that a solid base is needed for the stunt to work, and not everyone can be on top.

In this one particular squad I had several girls capable of doing the stunt. I chose one girl as the flyer and then assigned the other spots. Little did I know that her best friend had her heart set on the premier place in this particular pep rally. You can see where this is going.

As a result of not getting her desired spot, she turned on her "best friend." Even though I was the one who made the call, she was fuming at her friend for accepting the spot. Later I overheard her making weekend plans and intentionally excluding her friend. I even heard her making snide comments about her friend to the other cheerleaders. Sadly and ironically, this was supposed to be her "best friend," the one that she'd boasted about their bond and loyalty to each other. It seems their bond was shakable after all.

What I found so interesting was how justified she felt in her meanness when she didn't get what she wanted. Instead of being happy for her friend, she was jealous and angry. Instead of dealing with those negative feelings, she turned against her friend. I think pride blinded her from seeing why she was treating her friend so horribly.

Lest we believe that high school cheerleaders are the only ones who struggle with pride, we must think again! Pride is the root cause of most friendship drama. Ultimately our sin nature craves to be noticed, applauded, praised, and made much of . . . to be the girl at the top of the cheer stunt and feel deep resentment if we're not. Whether pride is garbed in a robe of insecurity and low self-esteem or dressed up in the finery of arrogance and false confidence, both are cut from the same cloth: a heart and mind focused on self.

In direct contrast to pride, the Holy Spirit directs us to think and act like Jesus. I absolutely love Eugene Peterson's translation of Philippians 2:1–8 in *The Message*. He so beautifully articulates the differences between our sinful nature, which is filled with pride, and the love of Christ, which is marked by humility and selflessness.

> *Whether pride is garbed in a robe of insecurity and low self-esteem or dressed up in the finery of arrogance and false confidence, both are cut from the same cloth.*

If you've gotten anything at all out of following Christ, if his love has made any difference in your life, if being in a community of the Spirit means anything to you, if you have a heart, if you care—then do me a favor: *Agree with each other, love each other, be deep-spirited friends. Don't push your way to the front; don't sweet-talk your way to the top. Put yourself aside, and help others get ahead.* Don't be obsessed with getting your own advantage. Forget yourselves long enough to lend a helping hand.

Think of yourselves the way Christ Jesus thought of himself. He had equal status with God but *didn't think so much of himself* that he had to cling to the advantages of that status no matter what. Not at all. When the time came, he set aside the privileges of deity and took on the status of a slave, became human! Having become human, he stayed human. It was an incredibly humbling process. He didn't claim special privileges. Instead, *he lived a selfless, obedient life and then died a selfless, obedient death*—and the worst kind of death at that—a crucifixion. (Phil. 2:1–8 MSG, author emphasis)

The selfless love of Jesus flies in the face of the world's self-seeking philosophy. Our culture embraces pride as a virtue. "Look out for number one" is the motto of this generation, and pride will run over anyone who dares get in its way.

Here are a few ways pride can manifest itself in friendships:

- Pride gets jealous and angry if a friend gets engaged, married, promoted, or pregnant first . . . although it will probably still throw her a fabulous shower.
- Pride gets hurt easily when not invited, not noticed, or not mentioned . . . although it would NEVER dare admit this fact.
- Pride gets sullen or snappy if it doesn't get its way . . . although it may accuse the other person of acting selfishly.

- Pride gossips about a friend in order to make itself look superior . . . although it more than likely would call the information a "prayer request."

As Christ followers, with His Spirit living within us, we must cast aside the pride that hinders our relationships and choose the way of Jesus, the way of humility. Start today with this simple confession: "It's not about me." We will talk more specifically about how to apply this truth in our friendships in future chapters, but for now we must recognize that the temptation to put ourselves first lies within all of us.

Envy

The distance between us grew more apparent over the months. At first, I chalked up the lack of communication to the inevitable change that occurs when one friend is married with children and the other is not. Since friendships are extremely important to me and I place a high value on time, connection, and communication, the distance was painful for me. She was not just any friend but one with whom I'd shared some of the hardest seasons of life. Then, seemingly out of nowhere, she seemed to withdraw.

As most girls would do in the midst of a friendship struggle, I took inventory: *Did I do something? Did I say something? Did I forget her birthday?* No, no, and no. For the life of me, I could not comprehend why I felt such coldness from my friend and why our interactions grew tenser each time we were together.

Since communication is key, I asked her what was going on. At first, she gave the typical excuses of "I'm so busy" and "life is just hectic." These answers made sense on one hand because they were true. We were both busy. But this answer didn't quiet the lingering question in my heart. I still felt something was amiss. The air between us just felt different. Time didn't make things better, actually, just more awkward.

Then one day she called. My friend is a godly woman. She loves Jesus and she listens to His voice. She asked me over for lunch and made a humble and frank confession. *She was jealous.*

Honestly her words were unbelievable to me. Ironically she was the one who was living *my* dream life. After all, I'd written books about my struggle with singleness and the pain of waiting on God for marriage, and here is one of my closest friends, who's blessed with everything I've ever wanted, and *she* is the one confessing jealousy toward *me*? It didn't make sense. Then I realized, envy can strike anyone, even the girl you think has it all.

Over a few months prior, the "have-nots" in both of our lives had created a chasm. I longed for her life, and she desired certain aspects of mine. Instead of honestly confessing the issue, we chose to withdraw from each other, which alienated us from a relationship we both needed and loved.

Joy Carroll, in her book *The Fabric of Friendship*, has a strong word about envy.

> The word *envy* comes from the Latin word *invidere*—to look hatefully at someone. Envy is having a strong, perhaps hateful, desire for the privileges, position, possession, or characteristics that another person has. If you envy a female friend, you want what she has and you think you don't have: her success, her looks, her friends, her money, her family, her man, her home. Envy can sneak into any kind of relationship and wreak havoc. It is a notorious killer of women's friendships. . . . Sometimes when we look at another woman's life, we make assumptions that her life is better than what ours could possibly be. We imagine that she has what is lacking in our life. We may get upset, even angry with her and with ourselves.[1]

Here we see the old sinful nature at work again. Envy says, "I'm entitled to what she has." This, too, is pride at work. Pride insists that we deserve something and is angry if it isn't had. A thankful and content heart is the antidote, but instead of trusting God and thanking Him for our blessings, our sinful nature becomes resentful and critical of the one who has what we desire. Truly jealousy is a poison.

Most of the time our response to jealousy is to cast a dark shadow on the one we envy. Our hearts turn from questioning, "Why not me?" to accusingly saying, "Why her?" If envy has its way, the one who has what we desire is treated as the enemy instead of as the friend, producing a critical spirit, avoidance of the one who is envied, and self-pity. Joy Carroll concludes:

> In attempting to conceal our envy, we may try one of many possible schemes—mostly unsuccessfully, I might add. Some of the most commonly used methods are what I think of as the easy "cheap shots": disapproval, criticism, gossip, backstabbing. We find a flaw or weakness in a woman we envy. By talking with others about her faults and devaluing her, we try to make ourselves look more important and her less so. For a while, we may even feel more powerful. We criticize a woman as a way of undermining her.[2]

Everything from cattiness to gossip can be traced back to this one source. The Bible speaks plainly to this problem:

> Where do you think all these appalling wars and quarrels come from? Do you think they just happen? Think again. They come about because you want your own way, and fight for it deep inside

yourselves. You lust for what you don't have and are willing to kill to get it. You want what isn't yours and will risk violence to get your hands on it. (James 4:1–2 MSG)

Most women don't enjoy feeling jealous of a friend, so instead of dealing with the envy, we opt simply to avoid the person. Consequently, when we withdraw, we suffer silently and alone. Envy divides. Envy destroys. The protective walls we put up in order to avoid feelings of jealousy ultimately tear the friendship down. We have a choice. Jealousy doesn't have to win. We can choose to address our sin and love our friend. We don't have to let the enemy destroy the friendship. His agenda to steal, kill, and destroy can be quickly exposed and dismantled if we choose to run to Jesus, confess our sin, and allow Him to pour His grace into our hearts.

That's why I'm so proud of my friend for addressing the enemy of envy and slaying it with truth. Her confession not only healed our friendship, but it also broke the power of envy. My friend recognized that I was not the foe, but Satan was our mutual enemy. He attempted to use envy as a means of dividing a strong, Jesus-based friendship. Her humility and honest communication healed the rift and proved to make our friendship stronger.

Submit yourselves, then, to God. Resist the devil, and he will flee from you. Come near to God and he

will come near to you. Wash your hands, you sinners, and purify your hearts, you double-minded.
Grieve, mourn and wail. Change your laughter to
mourning and your joy to gloom. Humble yourselves before the Lord, and he will lift you up.
(James 4:7–10 NIV)

We will discuss more in future chapters about healing
troubled friendships and how joyfully to defeat envy. For
now, if envy is causing anger, resentment, or cattiness in
any of your relationships, then don't just let the enemy win;
take action. Confess the sin of envy to Jesus and ask Him
to help you slay the green-eyed monster.

Competition

Competition is yet another way pride manifests itself
and can creep in and destroy a friendship. The desire to
be first, to be the best, to be number one is divisive. My
friend Shelly shared with me a painful testimony of how
this sinful desire shattered one of her closest friendships.

Competition destroyed my oldest and dearest childhood friendship. Julie and I first met in fourth
grade. We were the last two girls standing in an
audition for our school's rendition of the musical
Snow White. The problem was Julie neither sang
nor danced, but with her petite frame, blue eyes,
and black hair, she looked the part. I, on the other

hand, was singing in my crib and had been in dance classes since I could walk. Even with my blonde hair, I landed the role of Snow White. I should have seen this as a warning sign of things to come. Competition started early for us. . . . It was the unspoken elephant in the room from the beginning. While Julie was an excellent athlete and a great cheerleader, she desired more than anything to be on stage. I, on the other hand, didn't have an athletic bone in my body, but I could sing.

We became "best friends" in sixth grade. Our friendship cemented over flat chests and skinny legs. At a whopping seventy-five pounds each, we were the two smallest girls in our grade. We took turns defending each other from the taunts of middle school boys. Ironically, I never would have dreamed that one day we would need defending from each other.

Like most best friends, we did EVERYTHING together: slumber parties, family vacations, birthday parties, church camp, and Sunday school. This was also our biggest problem: we did *everything* together. . . . This included auditioning for every school play, musical, dance team, and church solo. Looking back, I so wish someone had told us that we could have excelled in different arenas and still maintained a close friendship, but for some reason we continually auditioned for the same roles. And whenever I was picked, resentment and rivalry deepened—although it was never acknowledged, of course!

Honestly, I'll confess, I wasn't extremely humble about winning these parts either. I'll own my sin. I found subtle ways to rub it in her face that I was a singer and dancer and she was not. While I wasn't overtly gloating, I did make statements that I'm sure didn't help to ease our competitiveness.

Although I would describe the friendship as "tense" at times, we did have fun and managed to stick together year after year. We would each make new friends but always called each other our "best friend."

We went off to college and decided to live together. Looking back, this was a huge mistake. College only intensified our problem. I was dying to spread my wings and meet tons of new friends and date. This new social scene brought a whole new arena of competition: popularity and boys. It was like we measured our status and standing by each other. If she was asked to a fraternity party, then I needed to be asked too. If I made a new group of girlfriends, then she needed to become more popular with them than me.

Competition became the air we breathed.

Eventually the tension and anger grew to a boiling point. We began fighting intensely and arguing all the time. Although our friendship was hanging by threads and we barely spoke, for some weird reason we still considered each other our best friend and tried to stay connected.

Then one day I was forced to face the fact: we weren't really friends anymore. I couldn't trust her and she didn't like me. I learned this fact from a guy friend who knew us both really well.

I met up with this guy for lunch one day after class. Julie's name came up, and I said that we were going through a rough patch in our friendship. He looked at me and said, "Can I be honest with you? Your best friend doesn't even like you. You know that, right?" I'd never thought of it so bluntly, but he was right. I began to cry. I asked him what led him to say this to me. He said that when I wasn't around and someone said something negative about me, Julie would join in the conversation and tear me down in front of a group of people. She loved any opportunity to disclose my faults and failures. The saddest part was he told me that when she heard I didn't get picked for an audition or win an award, my "best friend" would call him up and exclaim with excitement, "Guess what! Shelley lost!" My failures gave her joy.

It took a guy sitting me down and speaking truth to me for me to realize that competition had destroyed my closest friendship.

I'm sure each of us can relate to this story. While what we compete over may vary, we've all experienced the toll competition can take on a friendship. In a quick review of my friendships, I recognize that everything from a girl's jean size to her marital status could be in the arena for competitive games.

We tend to compete over the thing that we have chosen to define us. Let me rephrase that: we compete over the thing (person, possession, popularity, title, or talent) we think gives us our worth. If we tend to find our value in friendships, then we will compete to be number one in our friend circle. If we find our value in our physical bodies, then we will measure our worth by feeling prettier than our friend. If we find our worth in male attention, we will compete with other girls to get noticed by guys. If a mom finds her identity in the beauty, brains, or behavior of her child, then she will be highly offended or hurt if her child is overlooked.

Unquestionably girls and women compete with each other for many reasons: popularity, attention, recognition, men, promotions on the job, status, power. Sometimes in highly competitive situations, they are capable of becoming cruel, domineering, dishonest, and hateful. . . .

The amazing thing is that no matter the girls' race, geographic location, class, or religion, I always get the same answers. . . . They're all about competition, about looks, about style, friends, popularity, and boys—things girls think they need to secure a place in the life raft.[3]

Competition is sneaky. The temptation to compete for prominence grabs a girl by the throat and chokes the good sense right out of her head and causes a normally sweet and kind woman to act and react in ways that are far from Christlike. The fruit of a competitive spirit can be anger, jealousy, gossip, resentment, judgmental attitude, or a passive-aggressive withdrawal from the relationship.

Yep, this goes back to where we started: pride. This chief of all sins wants to be the prettiest, the smartest, the fastest, and even the most spiritual; consequently, we have friction with the person who threatens our perceived standing. Competing in friendship is like one of those ghastly mud fights on reality TV. So demeaning! We have a choice. We don't have to jump

> *T*he fruit of a competitive spirit can be anger, jealousy, gossip, resentment, judgmental attitude, or a passive-aggressive withdrawal from the relationship.

in the mud and make fools of ourselves. Repeat after me: DO. NOT. JUMP. IN. THE. MUD!

Competition is also rooted in insecurity. The essence of competition is that we are attempting to draw our security from unreliable and unpredictable sources. Whatever gives you confidence or wherever you are drawing your personal worth is what you and I will likely compete over. Our only solution is to draw confidence from Christ.

Just think about it. The woman who finds her security from her appearance will always struggle with confidence because the reality is that there will always be a prettier, younger, or thinner girl. Hence, the likelihood that she will feel competitive is also highly probable. Can't you see how insecurity breeds competition and how that can strike a blow to a friendship? In order to have real and lasting friendships, we must acknowledge the areas where we attempt to find our worth and security other than in Him. These places will serve as areas of competition and ultimately as places of division if left unchecked. The solution to insecure competition is secure confidence in Christ.[4]

The apostle Paul gives us a great picture of forsaking confidence in anything other than Jesus. In Philippians, Paul describes his spiritual resume—the things he could easily use to compare himself with others and the credentials he could easily think would give his life worth and value—as trash. Instead of trusting in these, Paul trusts in Jesus.

The very *credentials* these people are waving around as something special, I'm tearing up and throwing out with the trash—along with everything else I used to take credit for. And why? Because of Christ. Yes, *all the things I once thought were so important are gone from my life. Compared to the high privilege of knowing Christ Jesus* as my Master, firsthand, everything I once thought I had going for me is insignificant—dog dung. I've dumped it all in the trash so that I could embrace Christ and be embraced by him. I didn't want some petty, inferior brand of righteousness that comes from keeping a list of rules when I could get the robust kind that comes from trusting Christ—God's righteousness.

I gave up all that inferior stuff so I could know Christ personally, experience his resurrection power, be a partner in his suffering, and go all the way with him to death itself. If there was any way to get in on the resurrection from the dead, I wanted to do it.

I'm not saying that I have this all together, that I have it made. But I am well on my way, reaching out for Christ, who has so wondrously reached out for me. Friends, don't get me wrong: By no means do I count myself an expert in all of this, but I've got my eye on the goal, where God is beckoning us onward—to Jesus. I'm off and running, and I'm not turning back. (Phil. 3:7–14 MSG, author emphasis)

In order to stop competing with other women, we must stop comparing. C. S. Lewis once said, "Comparison is the thief of joy."[5] So true! When we eyeball our friend and think, *I should have what she has*, we set ourselves up for misery. Instead, we must turn our eyes toward Jesus. If we are looking to Christ and trusting Him for our identity, then our questions about our value become answered in Him.

The problem arises when we turn from Him and place our hope in other things. When our hope lies in these "credentials" that we use to make ourselves feel special, then we will struggle with competition. The bottom line is that our competitiveness within friendships occurs simply because we use one another as a measuring stick to determine our standing, our worth, and our value. Freedom from this snare happens when Christ consumes our hearts and we place our confidence in who He is. As the old hymn says, "My hope is built on nothing less than Jesus' blood and righteousness."[6]

*O*nly when we choose to deal with our baggage do we experience the freedom and joy in friendship that God intends.

Deal with Your Sinful Baggage

We all deal with the heavy baggage of a sinful

nature. Not one of us is free from the temptations of pride, envy, or competition. The choice we must make when tempted or caught in friendship conflict is this: Will we lay down the baggage, or let it divide us? Just as I had to remove my backpack when stuck in the elevator in Rome, we must choose to take off the old sinful nature and put on Christ. Only when we choose to deal with our baggage do we experience the freedom and joy in friendship that God intends. Friends,

> Let us throw off everything that hinders and the sin that so easily entangles, and let us run with perseverance the race marked out for us. Let us fix our eyes on Jesus, the author and perfecter of our faith, who for the joy set before him endured the cross, scorning its shame, and sat down at the right hand of the throne of God. (Heb. 12:1–2 NIV)

➡ Girlfriend Guidebook Tip ⬅

Let's all stop and take a quick evaluation. Has pride, competition, or jealousy driven a wedge or caused damage in any of your friendships? Do you find yourself dealing with any of the negative fruits? If so, acknowledge the problem, confess the sin, and fix your eyes on Jesus!

Everyone's got emotional baggage;
The question is, what are you doing to unpack
that trunk and put it away, so your lovers, friends
and relatives don't have to keep tripping over it?

—Shari Schreiber

CHAPTER 5

Deal with Your Baggage: Part II

Avoiding Baggage Fees from Unhealed Wounds

"That'll be $150," said the airline representative as I stood, staring at her incredulously with my mouth gaping open.

One hundred and fifty dollars?

Seriously?

"You've got to be kidding me!"

"Oh no, I'm not kidding." She quipped, pointing to a plaque behind her stating, the baggage fees. "Brand-new airline policy. Each checked bag now costs $50 . . . and well, seeing as both of yours are . . . *ahem* . . . slightly overweight, that's an extra $25 per bag, which brings us to, yep . . . $150."

Trying my best to hold my tongue, and recognize the fact that this woman was simply the messenger, I took a deep breath, closed my eyes, handed over my credit card, and quickly vowed to never fly this airline again!

Baggage Fees

As we all know, a girl needs her accessories, and a great bag is essential to any outfit. Trust me, I am the first to admit that I have all sorts of bags hanging in my closet: handbags in a rainbow of colors, backpacks galore, luggage in every possible shape and size, computer carriers for work trips, and cute little clutches for evenings out. Oh, the list could go on. But there is a certain kind of baggage that doesn't flatter anyone. I'm referring to the baggage we all carry that is more emotional in nature. It is the kind that jacks up our relationships and leaves us jammed up when we get close to people. This is our relational baggage.

There's a huge problem with our baggage—the fees! For the record I'm so over baggage fees! When traveling, which I do often, I do whatever it takes to work the system and avoid those ridiculous charges. Seriously, who can go overseas for ten days with a bag weighing less than fifty pounds? Not this girl! I think it's a secret plot against high-maintenance females. As I've said, I like my stuff, and I now have to pay extra just to have more shoe options? Insanity!

Likewise a heavy packer like myself gets penalized with fees by the lovely airlines, likewise, we, too, pay a high price when we carry baggage into our friendships. The price we pay is much greater, often costing us the closeness and depth of friendship we desire. Therefore, we can't afford not to deal with our baggage!

It's one thing to be a high-maintenance packer but quite another to be a high-maintenance friend. They are so draining, but more important these friendships don't glorify God! This is one of the biggest prices we pay if we don't deal with our baggage; our relationships don't glorify Jesus. Remember one of the primary reasons we need this guidebook is because we are meant to reflect Jesus to the world so that His life and love shine through us into the darkness. Trust me, if we don't deal with our baggage, we won't shine.

This nugget of truth hits a sensitive place in my heart that is still raw with pain and regret. A close friendship suffered because neither one of us dealt with our past hurts in a mature manner. The saddest part, aside from missing my friend, is that both of us love Jesus. Our friendship was meant to show the world God's love and grace, but instead we allowed our unhealed wounds and sinful responses to divide us, which resulted in a time of separation. God is slowly mending this friendship, but I still regret any ways that our conflict failed to glorify Him.

I don't know about you, but I want to be done with relational baggage fees! I may always have high-maintenance hair, but I don't want to be a high-maintenance friend. Freedom in friendship is found when we deal with our baggage. I can write about these issues because God led me to deal with my own. What about you? Are you ready to deal with yours? If so, let's start first by unloading the massive heavyweight that is our unhealed wounds.

Unhealed Wounds

> If we refuse to face the damage, the dysfunctional patterns set in motion to handle it [the painful events from our past] will continue to exacerbate the wound. Like a broken arm that is not properly set, it may fuse and heal improperly. We may learn to adapt to the way the fissures set, but it is unlikely to provide us with the optimum opportunity to live.[1]

My friend Mark shared with me a story that perfectly describes how our unhealed emotional wounds lead us to react in defensive and irrational responses in our relationships. At an elementary school that he passed frequently during his evening jog, there was an empty lot where kids played after school. One day he stumbled on the scene that absolutely broke his heart.

Jogging past the lot, he heard a whimper and turned his head just in time to see a small white cat, covered in blood, lying in the grass next to the sidewalk. Evidently some kids captured the cat and stuffed her body inside a ragged tin can and left her for dead. The sharp edges sliced open her stomach, and she bled profusely. Mark's heart went out to the poor little thing, and he tried to free her from the brutal cage and take her to the veterinarian. The problem was that whenever he came close, the cat freaked out, hissed, clawed, and fought him, injuring itself more.

Apparently the wounds inflicted on the cat left her fearful of any human contact, even from someone who just wanted to help. In his telling of the story, one statement stuck out to me: "You could tell the poor thing was in so much pain, but when I tried to free her, she unleashed her claws and fought me with all her might. . . . I guess she assumed I was going to hurt her again if I got too close."

Sadly many people react just like this cat in relationships. Unhealed wounds ring alarm bells, triggering our internal flight or fight mechanism, otherwise known as fear. If fear senses a potential threat similar to what has been experienced before, it will react. Like the wounded animal, we react defensively when people get close enough to hurt us, often alienating ourselves from potentially good and healing relationships. As Sandra Wilson says in her book *Hurt People Hurt People*:

> When we sense threats to our existence and well-being, we spontaneously act to protect and preserve our lives. For example, it's normal to run, hide, and even disguise our identity when we believe our lives are threatened. And we usually flinch and automatically protect a broken bone or raw physical wound when someone comes too close to it.

Similarly, in our sin-broken humanness, we normally adopt defensive, self-protective thinking and behavior patterns when we feel emotionally or relationally threatened and wounded.[2]

The problem with emotional wounds is that we rarely recognize when we have adopted the defensive, self-protective modes of operation. Often the people closest to us are more apt to see our patterns. Sadly, unless the wound is addressed and healed properly, it will continue to cause pain by alienating us from relationships and further preventing the intimacy our hearts desire. What types of unhealed wounds cause relational baggage? Here are just a few examples:

Abuse—The abused heart says, "People hurt me." Abuse occurs in many forms: verbal, physical, or sexual. A history of abuse causes victims to try to protect themselves from future harm, often closing down emotionally or withdrawing physically from relationships. Abuse can occur in a home environment or a school environment or anywhere in between. Angry, harsh, or critical words spoken by parents or mean taunts by bullies can both be constituted as verbal abuse. Sexual abuse ranges from inappropriate exposure to sexual content to something as devastating as rape. Violations may vary in degree, but emotional wounds resulting from abuse can drastically affect future relationships.

Abandonment—The abandoned heart says, "I'm all

alone. No one will be there for me." Abandonment occurs when someone is neglected emotionally or physically, if a primary caregiver abdicated responsibility (intentionally or unintentionally) or failed to protect and provide. Abandonment often occurs in children of trauma, of addictions, of divorce, or if a parent died. Divorced men and women also struggle with abandonment after their spouse ups and leaves. A history of abandonment may manifest in clinginess, neediness, or even a woman who is closed off emotionally to others.

Rejection—The rejected heart says, "I am not good enough." This lie stems from performance-based love in a home (if approval is given only when certain achievements are met), criticism from peers (the girl who suffers in shame from severe adolescent acne may feel unwanted and unlovable as an adult), or a romantic heartbreak (long after a person "moves on," the sting of rejection still lingers). A history of rejection causes a woman to misinterpret actions, project insecurities, and reject others before she can be rejected.

These wounds are real and legitimately cause pain. Relational baggage can result from wounds from early childhood or from a broken friendship last week. Regardless of when the pain occurred, if not addressed and brought to God for healing, the wound will fester and spread like infection to every aspect of our lives. As Wilson explains:

By "hurts" I mean actions, words, and attitudes that are intentional or unintentional, visible or invisible, hands-on or hands-off, other-perpetrated or self-inflicted, and barely survivable to hardly notice-able. The resulting wounds and injuries we usually call physical, sexual, emotional, intellectual, ver-bal, spiritual neglect or abuse. Most of this wound-ing neglect and abuse does not leave visible marks. Besides, even when these hurts create physical signs, bruises soon fade and casts come off eventu-ally. So in both cases, we may have only bloodless wounds and unseen soul-scars, some of which can last a lifetime.

When people try to function in areas that affect their untended wounds and unhealed hurts, they inevitably hurt others. Often they wound others as severely as they were hurt, and in remarkably similar ways. Who do they hurt? Usually, those nearest and dearest to them. To be sure, virtual strangers may superficially or profoundly wound us with their rudeness, their unprovoked violence, or in other ways. But our deepest wounds come at the hands of those we love and trust.[3]

Here are a few baggage behaviors that many women operate in because of their unhealed wounds. Now, before you read them, let me remind you to be reading with a lens toward seeing yourself and the baggage you need to overcome, not judging and labeling your friends!

The Fun Girl—Puts up emotional walls. Sally is fun and friendly but keeps conversation shallow; she doesn't feel safe letting people know "her stuff." While Sally is social, she doesn't like to get personal and expose her real self to others; therefore, she puts up walls to protect her heart from rejection. She thinks, *If they know the real me, they won't like me.* Sally's friends struggle to see past the facade and find the real her. True intimacy is stifled.

The Bolter—Walks away from friendships easily. Heather suffered from a deep wound of abandonment as a child stemming from her parents' divorce. Now as an adult, when she senses any type of conflict in a relationship, she withdraws and walks away from the friendship instead of dealing with issues in a mature manner. Her wounded heart's motto is, "Reject others before they reject you." She bolts when a friendship gets rocky.

The Egg Shell—Her moodiness keeps friends on edge. Diane's friends walk on eggshells around her, hoping not to set off her fragile emotions. One day she is angry, and the next she is crying. Diane's friends know she is easily offended and often hurt by small offenses. The truth is, Diane's unhealed wounds are so raw that normal relationship interactions brush up against a painful sore and she reacts out of the pain.

The Silent Treatment—Shuts down when disappointed. Allison is busy and forgets to return a phone call from Tiffany in a timely manner. As a result, Tiffany's feelings are hurt. The oversight hits the wound in her heart from childhood that said, "I'm not important." The two friends interact socially, and each time Tiffany is cold. After a few weeks of the silent treatment, Allison asks Tiffany about the distance but doesn't get a straight answer. Tiffany's typical behavior is to shut down when disappointed instead of addressing an issue maturely and telling her friend she was hurt.

The Porcupine—Keeps people at a distance. Brittany is quick to point out the faults in others in order to deflect attention from herself and to quiet the critical voice in her head. She uses a sharp tongue as a defense to keep people from getting close. This faultfinding nature drives away friends who receive the brunt of her defensiveness. In reality Brittany fears rejection and attempts to reject others before they can reject her. The porcupine tries to keep people at a distance because then she feels safe from harm. While the methods of distancing may vary, at the heart of the porcupine is the desire to keep her heart safe from further abandonment or rejection.

The Projector—Projects insecure emotions onto others. Trista walks into a meeting late where a group of acquaintances are seated having lunch. She hesitates at the door for a few minutes and then abruptly leaves, telling herself, *None of those women like me.* In reality, the women didn't even see her standing at the door. Trista simply projected her own feelings about herself and expectations of rejection onto the women.

The Siphon—Sucks the life out of her friends. Gena requires constant affirmation and attention from her friends. She demands a great deal of time and energy and barrages her friends with reminders of her existence via wall posts, texts, and phone calls. She is physically clingy and struggles with appropriate boundaries concerning personal space and communication. Her friends feel drained in her presence. Gena struggles with fears of abandonment and rejection and looks to others to feel accepted. (P. S. No one thinks they're the siphon.)

The Octopus—Acts possessive of her friends. Jill feels insecure and threatened if her friend doesn't have time to meet with her. She often acts jealous and possessive. Her heart fears abandonment and tries to prevent it by clinging tightly to her friends. She is apt to tell others who her BFF is and name-drops her BFF in conversation. When Jill's "best friend" forms a close friendship with another girl, Jill dislikes the new friend instead of accepting a third into their circle. The octopus looks to friends for security and will often overstep boundaries, invade space, and cling tightly to relationships.

The Monopolizer—Craves attention. In a social setting Tammy finds ways to turn the conversation back to herself. She continually talks about her troubles or her achievements and has little regard or interest in others. Her insecurity wants to be noticed. Her wound of rejection leaves her grasping for attention. This causes her friends to assume she's selfish when she's actually extremely insecure.

The Pretender—Puts on a false self. Jennifer forms a friendship with a group of girls from her gym. They run every afternoon and hang out on the weekends. These women attended prestigious universities and talk about their careers. Jennifer is insecure about her junior-college education and tells the group that she attended an out-of-state university. Embarrassed by her true background, she adopts a persona she believes will guarantee her acceptance into the group.

The Assumer—Struggles with insecure assumptions. Debbie sees her friend Stacy at church. Stacy is in a hurry and rushes past Debbie. Debbie assumes, "Stacy is mad at me. I wonder what I did?" She spends the rest of the day analyzing their friendship and assuming she did something wrong until her speculations turns to anger at her friend. In reality, Stacy didn't even see Debbie; she was rushing to the nursery because they had called about her son. The insecure assumptions created a division in their friendship even though Stacy is clueless about the whole situation.

Here's the truth: Because so many of us walk through life with unhealed wounds, baggage behavior is found

in nearly every relationship. It's
easy to see how these actions
and reactions would
render any friendship
high maintenance. Face
it, all of us—yes, *all of
us*—carry around some
degree of emotional
baggage. Each of these
scenarios began from a place
of pain but quickly turned into sin. It's

> *B*ecause so many
> of us walk through
> life with unhealed
> wounds, baggage
> behavior is found
> in nearly every
> relationship.

probably pretty easy to recognize the two-hundred-pound
pack your friend carries but harder to detect your own.
The temptation is to stop there, but as I've said before, the
one person we need to concentrate on fixing is the one
we see in the mirror. How do we unpack our emotional
baggage and walk in freedom? First, we must acknowledge
that we have baggage, and then we must entrust the wound
to Jesus for healing.

1. Own Your Baggage

We all have baggage behavior to some degree or
another. Those who recognize their own are best equipped
to sustain long-lasting, God-honoring friendships.
Knowing your own areas of hurt and weakness enables
you to stop blaming, finger pointing, nursing grudges,
and imagining offenses. If you're constantly dealing with

drama in friendships, whether you feel defensive, distant, or demanding, then it's best to take a step back and ask, "What am I carrying around from my past that may be causing these issues?" Taking an honest look at your past, your childhood, your sibling and parental relationships will shed some light on the beginnings of what I call baggage behavior. Take an honest look at your heart's deep need for love and acceptance and recognize where and when those needs were not met in your past; instead of projecting your pain onto friends, you can seek the healing from the Lord needed to give relationships the freedom they need to thrive.

For years I carried around my own unhealed wounds of rejection and abandonment. This pack might as well have tripled my body weight because of the toll it took on my relationships. Now, after years of Bible-based, Christian counseling and seeking the Lord for healing, I can tell you that these wounds resulted from painful events in my childhood. As a result, I was clingy and critical, jealous and insecure, full of assumptions and easily hurt. Oh, the drama! Thankfully, friends, I can say *I am not that girl anymore*! Jesus is not only my Savior, but He is also my Healer!

2. Entrust Your Wounded Heart to Jesus

"I will restore you to health and heal your wounds," declares the LORD. (Jer. 30:17 NIV)

Our emotional baggage is a big deal to God. He desires us to live in wholeness and freedom from our wounds. Scripture is filled with reminders that God alone is the One who can heal, restore, and renew our hearts. But we must choose to go to Him. In Jeremiah 30:17, the Lord specifically says that He will "restore" us to wholeness. In the original language, this verb is used in relation to a person's appearing before God. This verse conveys the idea that God is our Healer; our emotional restoration happens within the context of relationship with Him.

Jesus is our Great Physician, and He longs to heal your hurts and bandage your wounds. Isaiah 61:1, a prophetic passage about Christ, describes His life and ministry by saying that He will "bind up the brokenhearted" (NIV). The word *bind* in the original language literally means "to bandage, to cover, to enclose, to envelope." I love this picture. In it I see Christ taking the broken pieces of our lives and binding them together with His love and making them whole. But we must choose to go to Jesus with our hurting hearts to heal the infected wound and keep it from infecting others.

It would take more paper than Office Depot has in stock to write about my wounds that Christ has healed. When I first came into relationship with Jesus, I was a girl overflowing with bitterness. Honestly, I just thought it was normal to be angry, easily offended, untrusting, and critical of other people's faults. I had no idea these attitudes and actions were the fruit of a wounded heart. But soon after I surrendered my life to Christ, He started putting His Great Physician's finger into some of my old wounds and asking, "Does it hurt when I poke here?"

"Yeeeeees, that hurts!" I would scream, wanting to jump off the examining table. But Jesus continued to press. God revealed my unhealed wounds by allowing circumstances in my life to expose unresolved issues of rejection, abandonment, and shame. He used Scripture to speak truth to me about my sin that was rooted in bitterness, and He used godly friends to speak words of life to me. Dealing with unhealed wounds can be painful and, frankly, still isn't fun, but the process brings wholeness.

It is absolutely crucial that we deal with our unhealed wounds. Don't stuff the emotions down and pretend you're "fine." If pain goes unaddressed, it causes bitterness, which then poisons all of our relationships. So here's what I want you to do. Repeat after me these three statements:

I will deal with my baggage!

I will get real before God.

I will ask for help.

The "wound" could have occurred ten days ago or ten years ago. Either way, you need to let yourself deal with it. We get stuck emotionally when we choose to stuff instead of to heal. The result is a bitterness of heart that spills over into our relationships.

The Bible warns us about bitterness: "See to it that no one comes short of the grace of God; that no root of bitterness springing up causes trouble, and by it many be defiled" (Heb. 12:15 NASB). God explicitly warns us in Scripture that a "root of bitterness" causes trouble and defiles many. Imagine that a person's life is like a fruit tree. A tree contains a root system that digs into the ground. Roots provide life and nourishment for the tree. Fruit grows simply as the outward manifestation of the root. Now, if the root of a tree is bitter, what will the fruit of that tree taste like?

I know a girl who has not heeded this warning. Bitterness absolutely controls her, and as a result she has pushed away all of her friends. Her life is like a cup filled with a poisonous liquid. If people get close enough to bump into her "cup," the poison spills out and harms those around her. What happened to this girl? She experienced some horrific circumstances in her past: abuse, abandonment, and rejection. She chose anger, hatred, resentment, and unforgiveness. At this point she has not dealt with the root of bitterness in her soul, and the poison is literally destroying her body, mind, soul, and spirit—not to mention her relationships. She is extremely lonely but can't get past her pain to function in healthy relationships.

Now it is your turn. Perhaps you recognize a wound that affects your relationships. If you are ready to deal with the hurt, it's time to get real before God. Entrusting our wounded hearts to God requires pouring out the pain to Him in prayer.

I'll never forget the day I first unloaded my emotional baggage onto Jesus. I was serving on the prayer team at a women's conference. My duties included a huge name tag that read "Prayer Team." I felt so important.

That day, in an auditorium filled with hundreds of women, God spoke to me through the message and revealed areas of brokenness in my heart and exposed my unhealed wounds. Painful memories flooded my mind. The tears flowed down my cheeks and collected in a small wading pool on my collarbone. As most of my friends know all too well, I'm an obnoxious crier. It's not a small affair; it's actually brutal to watch. So, as I'm breaking down during the message, women begin passing tissues to me from all the tables surrounding me. Bless their sweet hearts!

I was a hot mess!

Here's where this story gets funny. As the speaker concluded her talk, she asked the prayer team—*that's me*—to report to the prayer room to "pray for others." Pulling myself together and wiping the mascara off my chin, I grabbed my Bible and reported for duty.

As if! Like I was in any shape to help someone else!

With all the dignity I could muster, I walked myself into the prayer room and looked around for anyone who needed healing prayer. At that moment I sensed the Lord whisper to my heart. . . . *Ahem.* . . . *Marian, it's you. You're the one who needs prayer.* I just hit my knees and began to cry out to God. About that time one of my friends walked in, discovered me on the floor, and knelt over me, praying as I poured out my heart to Jesus. For the first time I let out all the bitterness, anger, and pain that was lodged in my heart, and I gave it to the Lord.

What did I pray? Honestly, I can't remember the details. All I know is I was *real.* I laid down my baggage. I opened up about the events and circumstances that hurt me deeply and imagined my tears falling onto Jesus. I think my cry went something like this:

Jesus, I'm a mess! Please fix me.

Friends, this time of realness before God in prayer is only the first step. Healing occurs when we choose to forgive the wounds from our past and release the offenders to Jesus. The only way we will ever walk in freedom from bitterness is if we choose to release to Christ those who hurt and disappointed us. Otherwise, the anger and bitterness will fester and affect all other relationships.

A great description of forgiveness is found in Brenda Hunter's book, *In the Company of Women*: "I am no longer looking to the one who hurt me to make it up to me. I am not waiting for this person to change or apologize. I release them from having to make me OK. I make the decision to look to God to make things right in my life. The person who hurt me is no longer God in my life."[4]

Wise counsel helped me see that my wounds needed a season of Bible-based Christian counseling in order to heal fully. I can't stress enough how essential this step is for certain situations. Some wounds need special care. Sometimes we need help processing our pain and grief. Go to a trusted leader at your church and ask her or him to direct you to someone who can help with your specific situation.

Many of us have carried around relational baggage for so long we've become accustomed to it. The weight feels *normal*. A good Christian counselor will assist you in unpacking the load and help you learn new ways of relating to others in a healthy manner.

No More Baggage Fees!

As an experienced traveler, I've now discovered a few tricks of the trade that help me avoid those pesky baggage fees. I don't know about you, but I'd much rather save my money! In relationships, we, too, can avoid the baggage fees. We must recognize if or when our past is affecting our present relationships. If it is, then we must choose to take our pain to Jesus, get healing, and begin to operate within community in a mature manner.

Scripture admonishes us over and over again about the importance of maturity. While none of us can erase history and change the fact that we were abused, abandoned, or rejected, we do have a choice today as to whether we continue to live as victims and allow our past to define our future.

Friends, I have great news! Healing and freedom are available in Christ! Don't continue to pay the fees of broken friendships and relational drama. Deal with your baggage!

➡ Girlfriend Guidebook Tip ⬅

Change occurs when we grow tired of paying the relational baggage fees. Before moving forward to the next chapter, stop and pray. Ask God to show you if you have unhealed wounds from your past that are affecting your relationships. Ask a trusted friend if any of the patterns described in this chapter are evident in your life. Take the steps of healing outlined in this chapter and begin walking in wholeness.

Two are better than one, because they have a good return for their work: If one falls down, his friend can help him up. . . . A cord of three strands is not quickly broken.

—Ecclesiastes 4:9, 12b NIV

CHAPTER 6

The Top 10 Characteristics of a Christlike Friend

A travel guide just isn't a travel guide without a legit top ten list. Whether the destination is Austin or Hong Kong, any guide worth its salt will give the reader the "must see" spots and "can't miss" tourist attractions of a particular city. Trust me, as a frequent and *very* enthusiastic (ask my travel companions) tourist, I have tattered the pages of a guidebook from almost every city I have ever traveled. The thing I love about these lists and guides is that someone has already done the legwork for me. I can then coast on the coattails of the expert who has tried and rejected most of the possibilities and recommended only the best of each category.

So when I had eighteen hours in Paris, I did not meander through alleys, tunnels, and subpar patisseries. *Non, my cherie*! I delved into my Frommer's and dove into the city, eeking out every noble tower and infamous steeple along the Seine; fueled by *fantastique* French carbs and caffeine from the best croissants and cappuccinos the city has to offer.

So, basically girls, I love a list! Therefore, in writing and researching this guidebook on female friendships, I turned to God's Word to discover what the Bible says are the top characteristics of a good friend. Recognizing that God designed friendship with such beautiful purposes in mind, I figured He would have a few travel tips for us along the way.

Friendship is addressed over and over again throughout the Bible. With so much emphasis on the topic, we should pay close attention. The book of Proverbs, the New Testament epistles, and the life of Christ teach us godly principles for friendship. The night before Jesus' crucifixion, He gathered with His companions for the last supper. In this intimate setting, among His closest friends, Jesus disclosed that He would soon fulfill His mission to die for the sins of the world. In these final hours Christ shared a meal and shared His heart (John 13–14).

At the conclusion of this meal, Jesus rose from the table and asked the disciples to go with Him to the garden of Gethsemane. There, Jesus passed a vineyard, and picking up a grapevine, He illustrated the nature of a relationship between His disciples and Himself—the vital, life-giving nature a vine shares with a branch. Through this visual illustration, Jesus taught His disciples the importance of abiding in Him, but He also taught them a vital truth about friendship. He exhorts them to abide in Him and to follow His example.

> Abide in Me, and I in you. As the branch cannot bear fruit of itself unless it abides in the vine, so neither can you unless you abide in Me. I am the vine, you are the branches; he who abides in Me and I in him, he bears much fruit, for *apart from Me you can do nothing*. . . . This is My commandment, that you *love one another*, just as I have loved you. Greater love has no one than this, that one lay down his life for his friends. You are My friends if you do what I command you. (John 15:4–5, 12–14 NASB, author emphasis)

Just as a branch is fully dependent on the vine for life, the same holds true for you and me. Unless we are connected to Christ, drawing life from Him, we will not produce the godly fruit of love, joy, peace, patience, kindness, goodness, faithfulness, gentleness, and self-control (Gal. 5:22).

What does this mean for you and me today who live in a world where *Desperate Housewives* and *Gossip Girl* are our role models for female relationships? First, Scripture tell us to forsake a selfish culture and follow Christ's example of self*less* love. Our ability to love and befriend others comes directly from Jesus. He is the vine, and we are the branches. When we abide in Jesus and draw life from Him, He imparts to us the character and sacrificial love we need in our other relationships.

Godly character is the hallmark of a Christ follower, and this character leads us to treat others as Jesus would treat them. The following top ten characteristics of a good friend are found in the ultimate guide, God's Word. Each is an expression of Christ's character. As you read each of these traits, you may recognize many traits your friends have—just as glaringly as those that they don't have. But to have good friends we must be a good friend, so prayerfully read this list with yourself in mind. And don't sweat it if you have a few to work on. Simply ask the Lord to help you in those areas to model yourself after the ultimate friend, Jesus. Don't forget, Jesus is not only our role model but also our power source. Apart from Him we can do *nothing* (John 15:5)!

10. A Good Friend Is Loyal—*She doesn't throw her friend under the bus!*

Huddled together outside a train station in Sorrento, Italy, my "think tank" gathered to share and talk about female friendships. The thirty girls seated before me were college students from Ole Miss (the University of Mississippi). We'd traveled together for ten days on a mission trip in Italy and were at the tail end of our trip when I asked if they would take part in my survey. My first question was this: What character quality do you desire most in a friend?

From my vantage point I could see their eyes as they looked back and forth at one another before the first brave girl answered, "That's easy . . . *loyalty.*" Heads nodded in agreement all around me. There was a sense of knowing in all of their eyes, a look that said, "If a friend isn't loyal, then she's really not a friend." In a few of the faces, I recognized a different expression, *pain.* The lack of loyalty had left its mark.

As the weekend progressed, one by one they came up to me with their friendship tales and woes. Many girls have been deeply hurt by a friend's lack of loyalty. Their stories usually began with this statement: "My best friend threw me under the bus for . . ." As each story unfolded, I heard the heartbreak that the lack of loyalty caused. No wonder many are so skeptical of female friendships and prefer to hang out with the guys. The fact is, after trust is repeatedly broken, they had a tough time trusting girls.

> *A*ny person can be there for someone when it is beneficial, but a true friend is there when it's tough, when it's not popular, or when it costs her something.

What is a loyal friend? She is devoted, constant, steadfast, dependable, dedicated, unchanging, and unwavering. This is the friend who is there through thick and thin. Any person can be there for someone when it is beneficial, but a true friend is there when it's tough, when it's not popular, or when it costs her something.

The Bible describes loyalty this way: "A friend loves at *all times*, and a brother is born for adversity" (Prov. 17:17 NASB, author emphasis). Don't miss the key words "all times." Friendship isn't fickle. There is a sacrificial element to this kind of friendship. Former President Richard Nixon famously said, "What you learn when you fail is who your true friends are." Loyalty means we stand by our friends in good times and bad.

Les Parrott, author of *A Good Friend*, writes: "Faithfulness is the bedrock of any committed friendship. It gives the relationship the toughness to survive. That's probably why it seems so much more horrible that Jesus was betrayed by a friend than it would have been if a stranger turned him in."[1]

Ouch! With a kiss on the cheek, Jesus was betrayed by one of His closest friends. And for what? Money, power, and position. Judas traded Jesus for thirty pieces of silver. This is a powerful picture for us to contemplate. In friendship we often face opportunities to trade in a friend for something that benefits us. That benefit

> *O*ur friendships are meant to glorify God. For this reason, they will be put to the test.

could be a job promotion, a man, a place of prominence. Whatever tempts us to break loyalty, we need to stop and ask ourselves a tough question: Is this (guy, promotion, or thing) worth my friendship?

This point brings us back to our starting point: our friendships are meant to glorify God. For this reason they will be put to the test. Opportunities will arise when a friend seems dispensable, when you will be tempted to "throw her under the bus" in order to get ahead or to get the guy. Don't do it! Nothing speaks louder that we belong to Jesus than when we lay aside our selfish desires and choose what will bless, benefit, or protect another.

The self-seeking culture we live in treats friendship like a commodity that quickly becomes outdated when it doesn't benefit the user. Girls, this is not friendship as Jesus modeled it. Check your heart the next time you are tempted to toss a friendship aside or throw in the towel. Ask God to give you the grace to exhibit the loyalty of Christ to your friends and to be a woman who stays during good times and bad. Set your heart to be the kind of friend who stands by someone even when it requires sacrifice. Walter Winchell once said, "A friend is one who walks in when the world walks out." There is no greater way to show the love of Christ to our friends than by standing by them as a loyal and devoted friend. In summary, it's so not cool to be a Judas.

9. A Good Friend Is Trustworthy—*She keeps it in the vault!*

When I think of a trustworthy friend, the image of a bank vault always comes to mind. A vault is a place for valuables, for treasures, for items we want to keep safe. One of my favorite friendship phrases is when one girl looks to another girl and says, "It's in the vault." What this means, of course, is that what has been entrusted is "safe." When a friend shares a struggle or a trial, she expects that her private life will be kept, well, *private*.

The Bible repeatedly addresses the issue of gossip. Gossip is an act of opening the vault and giving away what has been entrusted to you. Not only is it hurtful, but it also leaves the victim feeling robbed of the valuable commodity of trust. Once again the Bible warns us against this temptation by saying, "Gossip separates close friends" (Prov. 16:28 NIV).

In previous chapters we examined various reasons we would be tempted to gossip about a friend: envy, competition, pride, jealousy, and our own unhealed wounds. One way we can overcome the temptation to gossip is to stop and ask ourselves a few quick questions to determine if the information is gossip or likely to hurt a friendship:

- Is it true?
- Is it necessary?
- Is it beneficial?

- Is my motive for sharing this information coming from a place of sin?
- Do I wish my friend good or harm?

"Do not let any unwholesome talk come out of your mouths, but only what is *helpful for building others up* according to their needs, that it may *benefit those who listen*" (Eph. 4:29 NIV, author emphasis). This verse instructs us to speak words that "build up" and "benefit" those who listen. The word picture here is the contrast between a demolition team that recklessly tears down a building with a wrecking ball and a construction crew that carefully uses tools and supplies to build something beautiful. We all must ask ourselves, *Which team will I work for—demolition or construction?* All of us desire the same thing: We want to encourage and bless people with our words, and thankfully, God gives us a clue as to how to do it.

The purpose of these questions is for us to evaluate whether we should say what is on the tip of our tongue. Let's imagine I have something I want to tell a friend. So I ask myself, *Is it true?* The answer: Yes. I know for certain that the information is correct. Second question, *Is it necessary?* Well, this is where I begin to hesitate. Sure, I could rationalize a reason my girlfriend should know the said piece of information, but is it really necessary? Suppose I determine it might be necessary for her to know, that brings us to the next question: *Is it beneficial?* No. No, it would not benefit her or the person being discussed for me to share the information. Therefore, I should remain silent.

Obviously we shouldn't talk about a friend if our motive is to hurt that person or her image. If this is the case, we've got bigger fishes to fry than gossip. We have bitterness, jealousy, or anger in our hearts that needs to be addressed. An example of this is when one girl makes a jab or snide comment about a friend in order to belittle her to others. These actions obviously aren't Christlike.

Trust me, I have blown it big time in my past. But over the years, when I've chosen to ask these questions before speaking, I've seen the benefit, blessing, and, yes, discipline of restraint. I've had fewer and fewer moments of regret. As it says in Proverbs, "When words are many, sin is not absent" (Prov. 10:19 NIV). The flip side of that coin is just as true: when words are few, regret is absent. By asking these simple questions, we can easily assess and hopefully stop ourselves from saying something that would ultimately break our friend's trust. A good rule of thumb is this, "Do to others what you would have them do to you" (Matt. 7:12 NIV). Girls, let's be the kind of friends who keep what is entrusted to us in the vault!

8. A Good Friend Is an Encourager—*She's got your back!*

Completely, utterly, totally depleted. No hope. I thought my life was over. My plan for my life was completely dashed—swirling in the toilet and flushing to a great wasteland of regret. Yep, that's how I felt about the breakup I was walking through. To escape my reality, I purchased a plane ticket to Australia to visit one of my best friends who lives Down Under. My plan was pretty simple. *If a girl's gotta be in pain, she might as well suffer somewhere exotic.* So I bought the ticket, ran to Target for last-minute travel toiletries, renewed my out-of-date passport, and hopped on a plane less than seventy-two hours after the most horrendous breakup of my life.

Little did I realize at the time that my painful circumstances were 100 percent in God's perfect plan, and He was orchestrating every detail for me to know His purpose and to redirect the course of my life. Since my friend lives in Sydney, we took the opportunity to attend a worship conference while I was in town. I didn't expect God to move in my life as dramatically as He did during that trip.

We attended the conference together, and while there, I heard clearly from the Lord that He wanted me to write a book about the show *Sex and the City* as a means of sharing Christ's love with women. Let me be clear about the context. I was desperately trying to eat solid foods and barely able to fake a smile, and God chose that stellar moment in time to call me to take a huge step of faith. Trust me, the only step I wanted to take was to the bathroom to chuck my lunch. Heartbroken doesn't begin to describe the pitiful state I was in—*and then God spoke.* The call was crystal clear, yet I was an emotional wreck and so full of fear and doubt that I balked. Thankfully, my friend was by my side the whole week, and she knew God was asking me to follow His lead.

If I'm honest with you, I think the breakup did a number on my self-esteem. Because when God called me, I told Him that He clearly had the wrong girl. I wasn't good for anyone—He needed to find another mouthpiece because mine was going to be busy crying for a few months.

Paralyzed with the fear of failure, I stood outside a Thai restaurant awaiting a table and downloaded to my friend all the reasons I couldn't do what God was asking me to do. Grabbing me by the arms, turning my face toward hers, she said, "You will do this. God is calling you to speak truth to women for His glory. Get over yourself and walk in obedience."

I so love that girl! I have no idea where I would be today without her words. She encouraged me with the fact that God would enable me to do what He was leading me to do. She continually spoke Scripture over my life and pointed me to God's great power. My friend saw past who I was in that moment (weak, unprepared, hurting, and broken), and she saw what God wanted to do and could do in my life.

Her actions remind me so much of Barnabas and the kind of friend he was to the apostle Paul. Paul came on the scene of Scripture as a man full of fury and determined to kill Christians. His life dramatically changed, however, after encountering the risen Christ. Paul was a new man with a new mission: telling others about Jesus.

There was a big problem with Paul's new mission and passion: the disciples didn't trust him or his newfound faith. They remembered all too well his old exploits and saw in him a man with a murderous past and an untrustworthy future. Their opinions changed, however, when Barnabas befriended Paul and brought him into the group of disciples. Barnabas didn't focus on Paul's past. He looked at Paul and saw what Jesus saw—a man redeemed and called of God (Acts 9:23–28).

The book of Acts gives a bit of insight into Barnabas. His name literally means "Son of Encouragement" (Acts 4:36). The word *encourage* comes from the Latin, which means "with faith." To encourage a friend means we choose to speak words of life and faith into her heart. We encourage with hope, with truth, and with confidence in God.

We are all meant to be a Barnabas to our friends—to see them as God sees them and to encourage that vision, to champion the cause of Christ in our friends and come alongside and cheer them on in their pursuit of His purposes. Friends, let us encourage one another! Build up your friends with God's truth and promises. Ask God to help you see your friends as He sees them and to speak His hope and strength into their lives.

7. A Good Friend Is Real—*She can't be bought in Chinatown!*

About once a year my girlfriends and I like to take a long weekend and go to "The City," otherwise known as Manhattan. Hands down, New York is the best place for a girls' getaway. NYC never disappoints.

Last fall I went with two of my best friends to New York. There's no greater time to visit the city. Central Park is ablaze with fall colors, and the sites and sounds of the holidays are beginning to transform the landscape. We visited our favorite places and discovered some new ones. Of course, no trip to The Big Apple is complete without a walk down the infamous Canal Street.

In case you haven't been, let me give you the scoop on Canal. Every label, every designer, every name-brand product can be found just south of The Villages in a little area called Chinatown. Here's the deal, though, while the name might read "Prada," or "Gucci," or "Fendi," it's not the real thing. Chinatown is the place people go to buy knockoffs to get an imitation for a fraction of the actual cost.

Let me say from the start, I'm not endorsing this business. Not only are the practices unethical, but the designers and manufacturers of the original purses, shoes, or watches are cheated by this industry. But, since I'm not writing a book to make a stand against counterfeit goods, let's get back to my point. Even though I don't buy from Chinatown, I still find it intriguing. The copycats go to great lengths to make a designer purse look like the real thing, but a discerning eye can easily spot the difference.

- *Prado* instead of *Prada*
- A Nike swoosh facing the wrong direction
- Kate *Spade* misspelled as Kate *Spode*

After just an hour on Canal Street, I always feel overwhelmed by the pleather. In a sea of imposters, I long for the real. The same holds true in friendships. It's easy to tell after a while if a friend isn't legit—if she doesn't let you know the real her. One of the most important characteristics of a good friend is authenticity. Authenticity makes us knowable, transparent, vulnerable, open, and honest.

People love the real thing. The problem is that our insecurity and shame cause many of us to try to hide, believing that if people really know us they won't accept us. So in an effort to mask our real selves, we pretend. We pretend to be fine when hurting or fabulous when falling apart. Our facades keep friends at a distance.

To have and to be a good friend we must be genuine. If we want to grow a relationship, we must let our guard down and let people see our hearts. Otherwise, the pretense prevents authentic community from growing. Jesus modeled transparency for us.

Unlike most gurus who have remained aloof from their disciples, he [Jesus] lived out his life squarely in their midst. Breaking bread with them, weeping with them, helping them resolve their quarrels, praying for them, he was intensely involved in their common life. Again and again he opened himself up to them, and when they did not understand him, he was grieved. To be sure that the disciples understood this deliberate self-disclosure, he told them: "I do not call you servants any longer, because the servant does not know what the master is doing; but I have called you friends, because I have made known to you everything that I have heard from my Father" (John 15:15). Transparency with one another, our Lord seems to be saying, signals that two acquaintances have become friends.[2]

How amazing it is to think that God opens His heart and shares His pain. Jesus wept. Jesus rejoiced. Jesus felt rejection and frustration. He revealed His heart to His companions, and from that transparency relationships deepened. Transparency is choosing to let others in and let them know the real you.

What does it mean to be authentic with our friends? It means allowing our friends to see both our failures and our fears. We remove the masks we wear and show vulnerability. This vulnerability creates intimacy and causes friendships to grow deeper over time. Alan McGinnis writes: "People with deep and lasting friendships may be introverts, extroverts, young, old, dull, intelligent, homely, good looking; but the one characteristic they all have in common is their lack of a facade. They have a certain transparency, allowing you to see what is in their hearts."[3]

I experienced this truth just this morning. I have a good friend who comes over in the mornings, and we exercise together. Over the last year our friendship has grown from mere acquaintances to a deep friendship. The reason our relationship has transformed is because of the heart-to-heart sharing we do. My friend and I talk. I mean, we *really* talk about the struggles and desires of our hearts. I've listened each month as she processes the fact that she still isn't pregnant and grapples with the fears associated with infertility. Her openness invites me in to know her heart. Because of this vulnerable communication, a strong friendship has developed. We've taken the time to get *real*, and the transparency in our relationship is amazing. I don't know about you, but I don't want a faux friend. I want the real thing.

6. A Good Friend Is Intentional—*She makes the effort to stay connected!*

Have you ever encountered a woman, who at one time was one of your best friends, and thought to yourself: *What in the world happened to that friendship? We used to be so close.* You two didn't fight or argue. You didn't split over baggage fees. Nope, the only answer could be the simple truth that you two drifted apart.

Drift seems to be the number-one cause of female friendship decline. There are a couple of reasons women slowly move away from each another. First, life guarantees change. In our fast-paced world change is constant. Just as the movement of a river erodes the bank, so the movement of life can erode the closeness of two friends.

Many common life transitions cause friendships to drift apart:

- Graduation
- Marriage
- Motherhood
- Pregnancy
- Infertility
- Career change
- Illness
- Death of a relative
- Geographical move
- Differences in income levels

Women undergo a series of profound transitions in the course of their lives. On average, graduates move six times after college, and the typical distance between friends is 895 miles.[4] In addition to geography, friendships are affected by new romances, new family members, and new career demands. Each of these scenarios can initiate the relational drift.

The reason many friendships drift apart is because few people take the initiative to stay connected. To plan actively and purposely to keep a friendship alive takes effort. Sometimes it feels easier just to let the relationship slip away.

So many women have asked me as I've researched and surveyed for this book, "How do I maintain a friendship in the midst of the pressure of life transitions?" One thing God has challenged me with in the last few years is to be intentional. Each day is a gift. Each relationship is a gift. Each new opportunity is a gift from God. My job is to learn how to manage and steward these blessings. This includes the gift of friendship.

Jesus modeled an intentional lifestyle. He knew His life purpose, and He lived each day on a mission. Jesus was also intentional about His relationships, and as Scripture reveals, He placed a high priority on them. Alan McGinnis observes this same character trait in those who are deeply loved: "As I've watched those who are deeply loved, I've noticed they all regard people as a basic source of happiness. Their companions are very important to them, and no matter how busy their schedule, they have developed a lifestyle and a way of dispensing their time that allows them to have several profound relationships. On the other hand, in talking to lonely persons I often discover that, though they lament their lack of close companions, they actually place little emphasis on the cultivation of friends."[5]

When we are blessed with a close, deep, and true friend, then we must be intentional about maintaining and cultivating that relationship. How do we do this? First, we must recognize that staying connected requires time. One thing God has challenged me to do is to be proactive and to plan for time to see my girlfriends. With the craziness of my ministry schedule, if I don't plan ahead for lunches, dinners, walks, coffees, and girls' night out, then I will wake up one day, nursing hurt feelings, and questioning why I never see my friends. In order to keep our relationships alive, we must be intentional with our time.

Les Parrott rightly attributes neglect as one of the leading causes of friendship drift: "Few actions speak more loudly about the value of a good friend than making time. After all, friendships today are in a cancerous state—undernourished, withering, dying—because few people take the time to keep them alive. They blame the demise on busy schedules, pressing deadlines, or geographical distance. But we all know that most failing friendships suffer from one ailment: neglect."[6]

The second aspect of intentional friendship is easy: Talk! This is one thing we do really well. To keep the friendship fires burning brightly, we must intentionally communicate and share what is going on in our lives. As I've mentioned, one of my best friends lives in Australia.

Even though she lives thousands of miles away, we have maintained a close friendship because of the amazing technology that is available. Once a week we video chat via the Internet and send e-mail updates as new developments occur. Honestly, this friend may know more about the issues of my heart than some of my girlfriends who live two miles away.

Here are a few practical ways to avoid friendship drift:

- Be the one who picks up the phone and makes the plans. Don't wait for your friends to call, to invite, to initiate time together.
- When life gets crazy busy, establish a monthly or quarterly girls' night. Set it on the calendar ahead of time so that everyone plans accordingly.
- Plan a weekend getaway or vacation with your best friends once a year.
- Multitask! If you need to run errands, invite a friend. A spontaneous trip to Target is a great girls' outing and is a great use of time.
- Married women, don't forget your single girlfriends. They still want to see you!
- Single women, don't forget your married girlfriends. They still want to see you!

With today's technology and travel accessibility, life transitions no longer need to signal the end of a good friendship. Be intentional! Take the steps and make the effort to spend time together and communicate.

5. A Good Friend Has Integrity—*She doesn't act shady!*

When my friend Jen sat me down at lunch to share her tale of a good friendship gone bad, she started her story with these words: "Everyone tried to warn me that she was acting shady."

Shady: an action that is questionable in nature and a teensy bit on the sketchy side.

If we aren't honest with our girlfriends, then we are acting shady. If we fudge the truth to make ourselves look better, then we are acting shady. For instance . . .

- Girls act shady when they make plans with a friend but don't commit in case they get a better deal. "Oh, I'm sorry, did we have plans for Friday night?"
- Girls act shady when they purposefully exclude a member of the group. "Oh, I'm sorry, I thought Betsy invited you. Did you not know we were going to the movie?"
- Girls act shady when they pretend they didn't get your text, your e-mail, or voice mail. "Oh, I'm sorry, my cell service is really bad here."
- Girls act shady when they have "selective amnesia." "Oh, I'm sorry. You were going to ask him to the date party? I sooooooo forgot. Oops."

The Bible says, "The man of integrity walks securely, but he who takes crooked paths will be found out" (Prov. 10:9 NIV). Ask God to make you a woman of honesty, a woman whose relationships are free of deception and duplicity and whose truth doesn't come in shades of grey.

Back to my friend Jennifer. It all started innocently enough. Her college boyfriend and her best friend met for lunch after class one day while Jen was away completing an internship. They felt a little awkward about telling Jen so they "failed to mention it" during normal conversations later that night. They weren't overtly lying, per se, just leaving out the detail. Neither wanted to admit that they probably enjoyed each other's company too much so they hid their now weekly lunch meetings from Jen. This minor deception opened the door. Soon they began hanging out more often, and their secret snowballed into an avalanche of lies. This shady tale is one we've all heard a thousand times—best friends divided over a boy.

The ironic part of this story is that her friend was a great girl, a real godly influence in her life, until her shady dealings with the guy brought an end to their close friendship. When faced with the temptation to deceive her friend, she chose the wrong path, and with that choice her integrity was sacrificed.

Integrity is living above reproach. It is a life marked by honesty and truthfulness. The opposite of integrity is deception and duplicity. Samuel Johnson said, "There can be no friendship without confidence and no confidence without integrity." When a woman lacks integrity, she will sacrifice her friendships to get ahead, to get a guy, to get noticed; essentially she will lie to herself and others to get what she desires most.

A good rule of thumb: If you are hiding something from a friend (that pertains to her), and it doesn't involve a surprise birthday party or future engagement, then you might be acting shady. Integrity is when our actions are open and honest and without deception.

Here's the bottom line: Jen's friend didn't act with integrity. She hid her actions and lied about her motives. The duplicity and double life resulted in severing a friendship that meant a great deal to both women.

4. A Good Friend Is Compassionate—*She walks a mile in her friend's stilettos!*

> Therefore, as God's chosen people, holy and dearly loved, clothe yourselves with compassion. (Col. 3:12 NIV)

The final four qualities of a good friend find their origins in a woman's relationship with Jesus Christ. As followers of Jesus—redeemed, forgiven, transformed, and dearly loved by God—we have the capacity, because of our relationship with Him, to extend God's heart to others—to befriend others as Christ would befriend them. A beautiful metaphor in the New Testament invites us to "take off" our old sinful nature, which is the baggage discussed in chapter 4, and to clothe ourselves with the nature of Christ. Applying this truth proves to be the key to becoming the type of friend that honors God and glorifies His name.

In the book of Colossians, Paul concludes his teaching about the supremacy of Jesus and the sufficiency of the cross by exhorting believers to "lay aside" the practices associated with a life focused on self and to "put on" the new self:

> Put on the new self who is being renewed to a true knowledge according to the image of the One who created him. . . . So, as those who have been chosen of God, holy and beloved, put on a heart of compassion, kindness, humility, gentleness and patience; bearing with one another, and forgiving each other, whoever has a complaint against anyone; just as the Lord forgave you, so also should you. Beyond all these things put on love, which is the perfect bond of unity. (Col. 3:10, 12–14 NASB)

A good friend is clothed with compassion. This character trait means she has a concern for the sufferings and misfortunes of others. This Latin word means "to suffer with" another. This is the essence of friendship: She hurts when a friend is hurting, and she extends the mercy and warmth of Christ to those in need.

So often friendships are based on having a good time. We equate friends with fun. True, I have a blast with my girlfriends. Just last night I belly laughed until tears rolled down my cheeks when a friend told stories from her childhood about being overweight and loving butter. (Yes, she would eat butter straight from the fridge.) So funny! Yet friendship is more than good times, good laughs, and full-fat butter.

True friendships are the ones that live in the trenches. Let's be honest: This world is tough. No one is immune to pain and suffering. For example, this morning I prayed with a friend who miscarried for the second time, another friend whose mother is battling cancer, a friend who is struggling to overcome a devastating breakup, a friend whose marriage is on the rocks, and yet another friend who is struggling with infertility.

Pain is everywhere. People are hurting. If we are going to be Christ to our friends, then we must develop compassion. Let me be frank and flat-out honest. I am not by nature an extremely compassionate person. I'm not one of those girls who cries at commercials or falls to pieces at YouTube videos about dying animals. Don't get me wrong, I do care. I hurt when my friends hurt, but I am not naturally prone to feel deep levels of empathy. Therefore, I pray for Christ to give me more compassion.

I ask God to help me "feel what others feel" and to befriend people in pain as He would. I often ask God to help me understand how a person feels and to relate to them accordingly: *Lord, help me walk a mile in her stilettos.* This prayer never fails. Compassion comes when I stop and ask myself: *What would it feel like to deal with* _____? *How would Jesus respond to a friend struggling with* _____?

Nothing speaks God's love louder than comfort and consolation from a good friend when walking through grief or experiencing a trial. Empathy and concern flow from God's heart through our hands and tears to bless and comfort those He has placed in our paths. Perhaps this is why Paul chose compassion as the first characteristic that we are to "put on" as followers of Christ. Compassion begins when we take our eyes off of ourselves and consider the needs and hurts of others. This is the life Jesus modeled for us:

- He walked in our shoes.
- He felt our pain.
- He experienced rejection, loneliness, and alienation.
- He wept for our brokenness.
- He is full of mercy and compassion.

Friends, let us follow Christ's example and lay aside selfish desires and clothe ourselves in compassion.

3. A Good Friend Is Kind—*She gives her friend the bigger cookie!*

Therefore, as God's chosen people, holy and dearly loved, clothe yourselves in . . . kindness. (Col. 3:12 NIV)

Kelsey, a young woman whom I disciple, flew in to visit me for the weekend in order to take part in an event for Redeemed Girl Ministries. Our day was jam-packed with meetings, preparation, planning, and executing the event. Throughout the day my phone rang with friends calling with encouraging words or last-minute reminders of the role they would play in the night. Arriving at the venue, we found ten of my best friends unloading boxes, decorating, cleaning, and getting all the details checked off for the evening's event. These women were beyond kind and generous. Each has a busy life of her own but graciously sacrificed to make the evening possible.

I was oblivious to the fact that Kelsey was taking note of my friends' acts of kindness until at the end of the night, she looked at me and said, "Wow, you are a really blessed woman. You have friends who would give you the bigger cookie."

What an expression of friendship! To "give the bigger cookie" is to sacrifice time and resources to show the simple gestures of kindness to one another. Kelsey was so right. I am incredibly blessed with amazing friends, women who put their words into actions and display the love of

Christ through tangible acts. One of my friends, with a full-blown migraine headache, spent the day decorating for the event without a word of complaint. I don't know about you, but I want to be the kind of friend who gives others the bigger cookie.

Recently I taught on godly friendships to a group of young women at my church. During that study one of my favorite female worship leaders joined us to lead praise and worship. At the end of the first night's lesson, she came up to me and made a confession. She said,

> Marian, I've got to be honest with you. At first, I didn't think this teaching series was relevant to me. I've kind of grown out of that girl drama stage, and my friendships are all pretty solid. But after hearing you describe the character qualities of a Christlike friend, I realized that not only is this the type of friend that I want, but it is the type of friend I need to be to others. God is calling me to follow Christ's example and serve my friends as He would, to love them as He would, and to reflect His glory in the way we relate to one another. Basically, what I hear God saying to me in this study is that I need to be a Christlike friend to the women He has put in my life. These girls aren't just here for social reasons, but God placed them in my life so I could both love and serve *them*.

Kindness is choosing actions that speak love. When we see our relationships through Jesus' eyes, we will begin to recognize opportunities God places before us to be the hands and feet of Christ to our friends. Acts of kindness can be anything from bringing food to a friend who is sick or surprising a girlfriend with a treat when she is blue.

When I was preparing to teach on kindness in friendship, I posted this question on Facebook: What is the kindest thing a friend has ever done for you? Here are a few of the responses:

I am a mom of a special-needs child. I recently began a new ministry at my church for these kids. Each Sunday I take them outside to the playground, and there isn't shade where we sit to meet. This Sunday I walked outside to discover that my best friend had purchased outdoor umbrellas for the playground. Her act of kindness spoke volumes. It said she believed in my ministry to these kids and she showed her support for me with her generous gift.

My best friend of twenty years patiently waited, patiently pursued, and patiently prayed for me to give up my life of addiction and surrender to Christ. It took seven years. Not once in all that time, despite my disastrous actions and behavior, did she ever make me feel less than loved. She was kind to me even when I didn't deserve her kindness.

After yet another negative pregnancy test and tears of disappointment, a friend showed up at my house with sweet tea and fried okra—my favorite comfort food! This friend has always been there to pray for me and with me. Hearing a friend intercede and pray to God on my behalf is one of the kindest acts.

Several years ago when my child died, I was a complete wreck. A precious friend from out of town hired a housekeeper to come to my house and clean. She knew I was barely functioning and that laundry and vacuuming were not at all on my priority list. That simple gesture has always resonated in my heart as God's love to me in a very broken season.

Girls, let us clothe ourselves in kindness. I challenge you to look around and seek out opportunities to extend gestures of kindness. When we actively love one another, we change the atmosphere of our environments. So much of this world is marked by competition and cattiness, gossip and greed. Therefore, when a woman of God goes out of her way to do a simple act of kindness, the beauty and glory of Christ shines into this world. Girls, let's glorify Jesus in our friendships by giving one another the bigger cookie!

2. A Good Friend Extends Grace and Forgiveness—*She meets her friend at the foot of the cross!*

> Therefore, as God's chosen people, holy and dearly loved, . . . bear with each other and forgive whatever grievances you may have against one another. Forgive as the Lord forgave you. (Col. 3:12–13 NIV)

Friendships can be flat-out frustrating sometimes! Whenever people are in relationships of any kind, conflicts arise. Some are petty and some are grand. The reality is this: For relationships to endure and thrive for the long run, we must extend grace and forgiveness to one another.

In Colossians 3, Paul makes a distinction between bearing with each other and forgiving one another. Bearing with one another is handling others' faults with grace and dealing with petty annoyances with patience. In friendship we will recognize quirks in one another's personalities that may cause frustration, but in these moments we must choose to "bear with each other." This is the essence of a grace-filled friendship.

Grace-filled friendships are a must! Goodness gracious, we all deal with crazy hormones, sleep deprivation, overwhelmed schedules, constant demands, and endless to-do lists. The last thing we need is demanding friendships that can't extend a sister a little grace when she's struggling to keep her head above water.

Too many good relationships fade because of some snub—real or imagined. Some people pout, brood, or blow up if their friend is not speedy enough in returning a phone call or if they are not included in a social event. They set such high standards for the relationship that they're constantly being disappointed. They can't let little things go. Every minor lapse becomes a major offense.[7]

Grace-filled friendships don't expect others to look, to act, and to think exactly the same. Such friends recognize that each person has a way of operating and responding that is different from their own. Bearing with one another means we let petty annoyances roll off our backs and put on the Christlike virtues of humility, gentleness, and patience.

Humility extends grace because it has the mind-set that says, "It's not about me." A humble person doesn't always expect everything to go her way. Gentleness extends grace with a controlled tongue. When tempted to lash out at annoyances or point out another's faults, gentleness will "bear with each other" with patience and will not be easily angered.

I once had a friend who would get mad at me because I responded and reacted to situations differently than she would. It dawned on me that she was angry because I wasn't *like* her. I was an extrovert and she an introvert. I was a quick decision-maker, and she was a slow decision-maker. I was spontaneous and she was calculated. True, our differences could be frustrating, but instead of embracing the fact that God wired us differently, I felt like she expected me to conform to her personality. This was not a grace-filled friendship.

While grace is for annoyances, forgiveness is for offenses. Offenses are the actions that hurt us (intentionally or unintentionally). In a Christian's life, forgiveness is not optional. Jesus said in Matthew 6:14–15, "If you forgive men when they sin against you, your heavenly Father will also forgive you. But if you do not forgive men their sins, your Father will not forgive your sins" (NIV).

As forgiven people, God expects us to release the offenses of others just as we have been released from our own debt of sin. In addition, Colossians 3:13 says we are to "forgive as the Lord forgave you" (NIV). I like to think of this as meeting the offender at the foot of the cross. When I place the cross before me and recognize my own sin, my own faults, and the many times I have failed to be a Christlike friend, it is easier for me to extend that forgiveness to another.

When I place the cross before me and recognize my own sin, . . . and the many times I have failed to be a Christlike friend, it is easier for me to extend that forgiveness to another.

Let's get real for a second. Forgiveness is for real *offenses*, the times when a person has wronged us or hurt us. If we are easily wounded and find ourselves continually at odds with friends, we may need to review previous chapters about unrealistic expectations and unhealed wounds. People will fail us and will not always meet our expectations of them. Having said this, forgiveness is for when we've been wronged, not just disappointed.

How do we recognize when we need to forgive? Here are a few questions to ask:

- Do you harbor ill feelings toward anyone?
- Do you rehearse speeches you would like to give to this person?
- Do you replay the offense in your mind?
- Is trust broken in the friendship? What offense broke that trust?
- Is it difficult to open up and share with this friend? When did this begin?
- Has a friendship ended without reconciliation? Why?

More than likely, after reading these questions, you recognize someone you need to forgive. Now what? Pray! In prayer, express to Jesus how the offense hurt you and damaged your friendship. Visualize your friend at the foot of the cross and extend to her the same forgiveness Christ has given to you. While you may not feel differently immediately or easily forget the wrong, there is power in forgiveness!

A word of caution: We must always forgive, but forgiveness does not always guarantee reconciliation. Reconciliation requires a repentant heart on the part of the friend who has done the wounding.[8] In the book *Grown-Up Girlfriends*, the authors discuss the difference between forgiveness and reconciliation:

> Forgiveness does not always bring reconciliation. If we choose to forgive our friend but she continues her behavior or refuses to acknowledge the pain she's caused, reconciliation may not happen. Reconciliation often requires repentance or changed behavior. If a friend wrongs you and does not repent, meaning she doesn't name the offense and behave differently to avoid committing the same offense again, you must figure out what God would have you to do. If the offense seems pretty severe, the friendship may be compromised or you may decide to move it to a different "basket" (category of friendship). Do pray about the situation, perhaps even talking about it with a counselor or writing out your thoughts. You might even take the risk of telling your friend that her lack of repentance seems to be coming between you and her.[9]

As stated many times before, it is far easier to see others' offenses but not as easy to recognize our own. If you have a friendship on the rocks, ask God to show you if *you* need to ask forgiveness for your part in the conflict. Ask the Holy Spirit to reveal any words, actions, or neglect that have contributed to the discord. Once again, humility and gentleness are required to own *our* sin and seek forgiveness when we've hurt another.

Forgiveness is the only way friendships can endure. Without this Christlike virtue, we will nurse grudges, entertain bitterness, and walk away easily when hurt. How better to show the world the love of Christ than to reach out with forgiveness when you've been wronged, to show the unconditional love of Jesus to the girl who gossiped about you, or to extend mercy to the one who betrayed you? Forgiveness evidences a supernatural love and grace that can only come from God above.

One of Jesus' closest friends, the apostle Peter, ended his letter to the early church with these words, "Above all, love each other deeply, because love covers over a multitude of sins" (1 Pet. 4:8 NIV). No one understands the grace and forgiveness of Christ better than Peter. After all, Peter denied Jesus. And in the end Jesus forgave Peter and welcomed him back into fellowship. How fitting then that Peter would teach us the vital connection between love and forgiveness.

Each one of us has been forgiven by our best friend, Jesus Christ. In response to His grace, take this moment to consider prayerfully any bitterness or anger still lodged in your heart toward a friend and release this person to Jesus.

1. A Good Friend Loves—*She seeks the best for others!*

I awakened this morning with this prayer on my lips: *Jesus, please teach me to love my friend as You love her.* I fell asleep the night before praying for this friend and for a struggle I see in her life. Staring at the ceiling, I kept asking myself that old cliché, *What would Jesus do?*

As I've stated time and again in this book, I am richly blessed with incredible girlfriends. Having said that, knowing how to respond and react to issues that arise is both complex and difficult. I struggle at times to know how Christ would respond to the various temperaments, circumstances, trials, and unhealed wounds found in each unique friendship. I'll be honest, discerning what "love" would do is a case-by-case and moment-by-moment decision to seek Jesus and ask for His heart and mind toward my friends.

Girls, it is imperative that we choose this route. The world tells us to walk away and give up when a friendship grows difficult or when facing bumps in the road. Yet the Bible repeatedly reminds us that *love* is the chief characteristic of a person who is in relationship with God. Therefore, in these moments we must ask ourselves, *What would love do in this situation?*

Love is the evidence that we know God. When we love one another as God loves us, this displays to the watching world that knowing and following Jesus truly does make a difference. That is why our friendships should be different from those who don't know God.

> My beloved friends, let us continue to love each other since love comes from God. Everyone who loves is born of God and experiences a relationship with God. The person who refuses to love doesn't know the first thing about God, because God is love—so you can't know him if you don't love. This is how God showed his love for us: God sent his only Son into the world so we might live through him. This is the kind of love we are talking about—not that we once upon a time loved God, but that he loved us and sent his Son as a sacrifice to clear away our sins and the damage they've done to our relationship with God.
>
> My dear, dear friends, if God loved us like this, we certainly ought to love each other. No one has seen God, ever. But if we love one another, God dwells deeply within us, and his love becomes complete in us—perfect love! (1 John 4:7–12 MSG)

As Christians, we no longer need to fight for acceptance, popularity, status, and prestige. We know that God has declared us loved, forgiven, and redeemed; and we can now lay down our agendas and choose to love one another as Christ loves us. A simple, yet profound definition for *love* is "seeking the best for others." This is the example Jesus set for us as described in Philippians:

> If you've gotten anything at all out of following Christ, if his love has made any difference in your life, if being in a community of the Spirit means anything to you, if you have a heart, if you care— then do me a favor: Agree with each other, love each other, be deep-spirited friends. Don't push your way to the front; don't sweet-talk your way to the top. Put yourself aside, and help others get ahead. Don't be obsessed with getting your own advantage. Forget yourselves long enough to lend a helping hand. (Phil. 2:1–4 MSG)

The bottom line is that love forgets itself and seeks the best for the other person. The baggage of jealousy, competition, envy, and pride no longer binds Christ followers. With hearts rooted and grounded in the truth that God lavishly loves us, we can now boldly love those He places before us.

*A*s Christians, we no longer need to fight for acceptance, popularity, status, and prestige. We know that God has declared us loved, forgiven, and redeemed.

So, what is the loving thing to do?

- Love listens.
- Love speaks truth to a friend, even when it is difficult.
- Love confronts the eating disorder.
- Love addresses the addiction.
- Love applauds victories.
- Love grieves losses.
- Love does not stand by passively while a friend rebels against God.
- Love defends.
- Love does not turn a blind eye to destructive practices.
- Love changes plans for a friend in need.
- Love desires God's best for another.
- Love sacrifices to help and to heal.

Knowing the answer to my question, I realize now what I must do. I must *love* her. Processing this situation, love means I overcome my fear and talk to her about the problem. Love means I value the well-being of my friend more than I do my own comfort. Love means I speak up.

Love has a different face in every situation, but it should always reflect the face of Jesus.

Love is patient, love is kind. It does not envy, it does not boast, it is not proud. It is not rude, it is not self-seeking, it is not easily angered, it keeps no record of wrongs. Love does not delight in evil but rejoices with the truth. It always protects, always trusts, always hopes, always perseveres.

Love never fails.

—Paul, 1 Corinthians 13:4–8 NIV

Kingdom Friendships: Traveling Together for the Glory of God

Sitting all alone in my postcollege, single-girl apartment, the truth dawned on me: *Life as I'd known it was over.* The new man in my life was changing everything. No longer was I the party girl, going out to clubs at night with friends with whom I shared the lofty goal of getting hammered and meeting hot guys. Now I was a different girl living for a different purpose. I was a redeemed girl living for her Redeemer. My life was radically different than it had been just weeks before.

In my early twenties, during my heyday in the party scene, I realized I wanted more. The intoxicating allure of the *Sex and the City* lifestyle left me empty and yearning for something that truly satisfied. I wanted *real* life. I found just that—life—when I came to the end of myself and recognized my need for Jesus. Receiving His gift of grace, I surrendered my life to Him. Yes, girls, the new man in my life was none other than Jesus Christ. And let me just say, for the record, Jesus changed everything.

One change I wasn't prepared for was the shift in my female friendships. As girls, we tend to live in a fantasyland where best friends are forever and first loves never fail. As we know, that only happens in Hollywood. I quickly realized that I had little in common with the girls I once called my "best friends." My bar-hopping days were behind me. Looking back, I realize that the common denominator in those relationships was the party scene; and once removed, it left a gaping void filled by awkward silences and forced small talk. Frankly, once I started following Jesus, I didn't have much in common with my old girlfriends. I didn't have a story to contribute to the morning-after breakfast since I wasn't part of the antics that had gone down the night before; therefore, the basis of our friendship (boys and bars) was gone. After a few weeks of trying to find something to talk about and attempting to build a connection, I found myself alone.

I was more than OK with the lifestyle change. Honestly, I'd lost the taste for that scene. I didn't mind being left out of the drama, but I wasn't prepared for the reality that my entire social life was wrapped up with those girls. My new social status, *solo*, didn't come easily for this naturally sanguine, people person. I'm not the kind of girl who craves alone time. I really like people. I would make a terrible monk. I love hanging out with friends, and I don't relish the idea of too much "me" time. So, when I found myself all alone on a Saturday night, that was fodder for some serious prayer (as in the on-my-face-begging-God-for-help kind of prayer).

I know this sounds a teensy bit selfish, but it wasn't a desire for world peace or disaster relief that sent me running to the throne of grace. Oh no!—my supplication wasn't that lofty. However, I was incredibly earnest and a tad bit desperate as I prayed for Christian friends who lived for the kingdom of God.

I knew myself well enough to admit that I was easily influenced by the company I kept. That being the case, I knew I desperately needed Christian girlfriends. As a new believer, my desire was to follow Jesus with my whole heart, but I couldn't do it alone; therefore, I prayed for friends with the same purpose and passion.

I distinctly remember sitting alone on my bed in that apartment, with my Bible and first devotional journal in hand, pouring out my heart to God and asking Him to provide Christian girlfriends. My journal entry reads as follows: "Please, Jesus, I can't do this Christian life alone. I need friends who love You. I know I will fall back into my old ways unless You give me new friends. I need girlfriends who want to live for You and to follow You in obedience."

The Bible says that our prayers move mountains and our Heavenly Father loves to provide for His children.

Trust me, this is a fact! I've seen it firsthand. Fast-forward to one decade later; I am one incredibly blessed woman.

I now sit in a hotel room at a fabulous resort. Instead of sitting alone, I am joined by three of my closest girlfriends, women who are sold-out for Christ and passionately serve His kingdom. These women are part of an accountability group I've met with for nearly ten years. This fabulous foursome met on a weekly basis to read God's Word, share struggles, and pray for one another. God used this time to transform and to sanctify each of us more into the image of Christ.

I can't recommend highly enough that women come together on a regular basis to strengthen their relationship with Christ. These friendships share a richness others will never know. The depth of love and transparency is unparalleled. The outcome of the time is nothing short of transformation.

The book of Proverbs illustrates this refining process by saying: "As iron sharpens iron, so one person sharpens another" (Prov. 27:17 NIV). That is the best description of our accountability group. We have been God's tool of refining and strengthening one another. We've been a safe place to confess sin as it says in 1 John 1:9, and we've loved one another enough to say, "This area of your life doesn't glorify God." The Bible says in Proverbs 27:6, "The wounds of a friend can be trusted" (NIV). This type of honest communication is the nature of the relationship we share. We love one another enough to speak truth, even when it hurts us to do so. And we've encouraged one another with promises from God's Word when one of us is walking through a tough season.

Right now we don't have the luxury of meeting once a week, but we do plan for regular times to connect, pray, and hold one another accountable. Our current weekend getaway was planned months in advance. We had to juggle four busy schedules, but we did it! Blessed with the luxury of uninterrupted time (no kids, no husbands, no deadlines), we can think of nothing better to do than pile on a bed and just talk for hours. Our treat on this retreat is simply time together—sharing, laughing, crying, and praying for one another. My mental snapshot of this moment is a precious memory, for within its frame is a picture of the beautiful gift God provided, amazing girlfriends who love Jesus with their whole hearts.

Breathing in this scene, I can't help but think how God has been more than good to me. He has been lavish in His gift of friends. I am awed and amazed at the godly Christian women He has placed in my life. Friends who have not only shared my passion for Jesus but loved me through the joys and sorrows, held me together, spoken truth in love, and celebrated the victories.

C. S. Lewis once said that friends are "side by side, absorbed in a common interest."[1] For a group of Christian friends, that common interest is Jesus Christ. The glue that binds through the tough times is His glory. The overarching purpose that encourages loyalty, forgiveness, and love is each person's desire to reflect Him to the world.

God has used friendships as a means of furthering His kingdom agenda since the beginning. Just think about it: The twelve disciples were a group of friends who followed Jesus and literally changed the world. Changed. The. World! Picking up their baton, the apostle Paul and his friends John Mark, Timothy, and Barnabas traveled together sharing Jesus with those they met. On one such journey Paul encountered Lydia, a successful businesswoman, and a group of her friends gathered for prayer by a river (Acts 16:11–15). Paul shared the gospel with them, and this group of women became the first followers of Christ in Europe! Centuries later a small group of friends praying together would spark the Great Awakening that would spread the gospel throughout England and North America.

Today I have the joy of traveling to college campuses and witnessing as college women and sorority sisters come together to see others at their university come to know Christ. Their friendships springboard into campus-wide awakenings!

Friends who are consumed with God's glory and running hard after Jesus can literally change the world. Remember, we are created by God and for God. Our friendships are not accidental but purposefully chosen by Him. Together we encourage and challenge one another to fulfill our kingdom purpose. When the common ground in a friendship is Jesus Christ, the relationship transforms from an ordinary friendship into a supernatural partnership. We are stewards of many things: money, time, talents, but also relationships.

God has entrusted friends to us for His glory. There is a high and holy purpose to these relationships. Think about it: What could God do through yours?

Kingdom Purpose

While studying abroad in Oxford, England, my dorm was just around the corner from the very spot where C. S. Lewis met with his close friends J. R. R. Tolkien, Charles Williams, and others in a group called The Inklings. Their favorite meeting spot was a pub called The Eagle and Child. One day I went there for lunch—ordering the obligatory fish and chips, of course. Finding a seat near the back by the fireplace, I took in the room and thought, *Wow, if these walls could talk.* In his letters Lewis once wrote, "Is any pleasure on earth as great as a circle of Christian friends by a fire?"[2]

Here by this fire, in this place, once sat a circle of friends. Some of the greatest works of literature in the last century were birthed from conversations that occurred between them. I can just imagine the day that Tolkien first told them the tale of a Hobbit, who, finding a special ring, set off on an amazing adventure. Could they have known that one day, sixty years later, grown men and women would flock to theaters, dressed like elves and hobbits, to watch *The Lord of the Rings*? Or what about the day Lewis shared with his friends about four children who stumble upon the magical land of Narnia. Did they have a clue that the chronicles they helped him craft would have such a profound influence on the Christian faith?

Just imagine . . . what if these friendships never happened?

Lewis grasped the magnitude of friendship. After all, he is the one who described God as the "Secret Master of Ceremonies," bringing individuals together as friends to accomplish His divine purpose. God used Tolkien to lead Lewis to faith, and in turn Lewis's writings have led millions to trust in Jesus. Truly their friendship was not a mere coincidence.

The same holds true for me and for you. Who we are friends with is not an accident. God's hand is at work. He not only created relationships; He also uses them to accomplish mighty works in and through us. Take a moment to thank God for your friends. Pray for each of them by name. Ask Jesus to accomplish His perfect will through these relationships. Ultimately, pray that through them Jesus Christ will be glorified and His kingdom advanced.

So, as you close the pages of this guidebook, focus on this truth: The "Secret Master of Ceremonies" is at work right now divinely moving in your circle of friends. Your friendships are not mere coincidental chaos, clashes of momentary laughter, fashion foibles, and silly secrets shared for this season only.

Is something much more profound stirring among your pounding hearts? Are the love and the loyalty, the tears and the fears part of a bigger purpose than you can even grasp? What kingdom agenda could God accomplish through your relationships? Has the Master of Ceremonies orchestrated friendships in your life that will send ripples of applause echoing into eternity?

Small-Group Questions

Chapter 1: The Girlfriend Guidebook

1. Who was your childhood best friend? What is your favorite friendship memory? Whom do you consider a close friend today?

2. Near the bottom of page 7, Marian says sometimes she feels like she needs a guidebook for girlfriend relationships. Can you relate? Have you ever felt you needed guidance in a particular instance/situation with a friend?

3. Have you ever failed or been the cause of a friendship breakup? Share if you feel comfortable.

4. On page 10, Marian says that few people actually know what the word *friend* means. What do you think of when you hear the word *friend*? What does a "good friend" look like to you?

5. On page 15, Marian mentions that friendship pains and misunderstandings are often swept under the rug. Think about your friendships. Have you swept under the rug any areas of hurt or misunderstanding? Are there areas

you didn't want to discuss or bring up but have really put a damper on your friendship?

6. Read the bottom of page 19. Who/what do you turn to first for guidance? The phone? Internet? Your mentor? Mother? Or do you first look to God and His Word?

7. Read through the questions Marian asks on page 21 and think through your friendships. Do you see any patterns in how you handle your relationships that may need to be looked into?

Chapter 2: The Destination

1. Page 30 gives us the definition of a friend. What characteristics do you look for in a friend?

2. Page 30 tells us that a friend is a "trustworthy peer." Let's examine ourselves. Am I a trustworthy friend? Are all things kept confidential? Or can I not wait to tell the next "friend" the story I just heard?

3. A friend is also a servant. Read through the description of a servant friend on page 32. Do any of your friends stand out to you as servants? Take time to thank them for being there for you!

4. Beginning on page 37, Marian mentions that friendships are a part of our sanctification. What do you think this means? How can friendships be part of our being sanctified to be more and more like Christ?

Chapter 3: The Perfect Travel Companion

1. This chapter describes a train wreck Marian experienced in Europe. Share stories of when a friend was there for you during a major "train wreck" in your life.

2. Page 47 talks about relational idolatry. Reread this section and ask yourself, *Do any of my friendships border on idolatry?*

3. Do you find yourself dwelling on whether your friends accept or approve of you? What is the underlying issue here?

4. Go through the questions on page 54 about relational idolatry. Is this a struggle?

5. On pages 56–57, Marian talks about how she repented of relational idolatry after train wrecking several of her friendships. Repentance always means change. Are you making steps to change your unhealthy patterns? If so, how?

6. Look at the section entitled "Reconnect with God's Truth" on page 58. We must know what God says about us. Read Psalm 139:13–16. What does this passage say about you? What does it say about God's acceptance and love for you?

Chapter 4: Deal with Your Baggage: Part I

1. Marian uses the illustration of baggage to describe friendship drama. How did this illustration help you examine your own friendships?

2. Page 71 begins the talk about pride and how it can be a huge destroyer of any relationship. Take a look at yourself. (NOT your friends!). How have you responded out of pride in a friendship? Do you always have to be the girl at the top of the cheer stunt?

3. Another relationship destroyer is envy. Examine yourself. Jealousy can manifest itself in just wanting something others have; or it can go much, much deeper and not only want what others have but also not want others to have it either! Do you sometimes wish that good would not come to your friend? Is that how a true friend should feel? Why do you think you feel that way?

4. Competition is another relationship obstacle. Do you compete against your friends in certain areas? Boys? Grades? Success? The areas you compete in are often what you are letting define you. What is defining you?

5. On page 90, Marian quotes C. S. Lewis: "Comparison is the thief of joy." What do you think about this statement? Can you see this is true in your friendships?

Chapter 5: Deal with Your Baggage: Part II

1. Read through the different baggage behaviors on pages 101–104. Do you see yourself in any of these types of girls?

2. Does a lot of drama surround your friendships? Do you think that you could be encouraging this type of drama by your past woundings?

3. Marian points out that we must deal with our baggage! Do any areas you have not dealt with come to mind? Areas where you have said, "I'm fine," and put on the smiling face, but deep inside you know something is wrong?

4. Marian says that she finally got real with God. Looking at the areas that need healing, are you ready to get real and take action? First, confess and ask God for help! Second, do you need to forgive and release anyone who has hurt you?

Chapter 6: The Top 10 Characteristics of a Christlike Friend

1. John 15:13 says, "Greater love has no one than this, that he lay down his life for his friends" (NIV). How do you as a friend lay down your life for others? Ask yourself, *Am I selfless or selfish in my friendships?*

2. One characteristic of a friend is loyalty. What times stand out when a friend showed her loyalty? How does that signify Christ to you?

3. Another characteristic is trustworthiness. Have you recently blown it by letting private information be known? Examine your motives. Does it point to some deeper hurt or "baggage" that has not been properly dealt with?

4. "Encouraging" is another characteristic of a friend. Do you have a friend who always encourages you? If so, thank her for that gift! Discuss ways you could be more encouraging to your friends.

5. A friend is real. Do you open up to your friends? Do they know your struggles and fears? What keeps you from opening up, from sharing your real hurts and pains?

6. A huge part of maintaining a friendship is being intentional. We must take time to stay connected. How does this relate to our time with God?

7. Extending grace and forgiveness is a necessary part of any friendship. Do you hold your friends to perfection? Do you get upset if they don't always act as you would? We are sinful, flawed people; if God can forgive you or your issues, can't you extend grace to your friends?

8. Read the questions Marian presents on page 149. Turn to 1 Corinthians 13:5 in your Bible. It says love does not keep any record of wrongs and is not easily offended. What does this mean?

Chapter 7: Kingdom Friendships

1. Marian talks about how, once she came to know Jesus, she didn't have anything in common with her old friends. Do you have "friends" from your old life that you just don't click with anymore? What was the common denominator in your friendship?

2. How are you handling these friendships now?

3. Look back through all of the areas of friendship discussed in this book. What area or areas stick out as those you need to work on most?

4. How can you be a better friend to accomplish God's purpose?

Acknowledgments

I am one incredibly blessed woman! Years ago when I prayed for Christian friends, little did I know that God would answer that prayer above and beyond my wildest imagination! God has been very good to me; this book is proof of His blessing.

To the Redeemed Girl Board of Directors (Matt and Jessica, Leti and Chaz, Jeff and Jenny, Geoff and Catherine, Ryan and Kim, Kitty, Anita, Leigh and Tonya: I am forever grateful for your support. You were my friends first, long before there was a ministry, and for that reason our service together is that much sweeter.

Jessica Trozzo: Thank you for the transparent conversation that inspired this book and for carefully reading every word. Your input and ideas were priceless. I love how you long for God's best in friendships. You've proven it with me time and again.

Catherine King: You are the epitome of a loyal friend. As I wrote the Top 10 List, I thought of you. Thank you for sacrificially giving your time to edit this book.

Angel Texada and Mimi Epps: Thank you for the friendship we share and for listening to these chapters (over and over again) with such patience and grace. Both of you are incredible examples of Christlike friendship. You fill my life with such joy.

To my travel companions, whose stories graced the pages of this book: Cristy, Christy, Jennifer, Keri, and Jamia. Thank you for letting me share our journeys. I'm especially grateful for our enduring friendships.

A special thanks to my home church, Second Baptist Church of Houston, Texas. Thank you for the privilege of serving Jesus and for allowing me the honor of teaching *The Girlfriends Guidebook* to women. Thank you Susanna Thorn and Inger Calderon for making that study so special. You are precious gifts from the Lord.

To my friends at B&H Publishing Group: I've loved working with you in furthering the kingdom. Thank you Haverly Pennington and Jennifer Lyle for all you do.

To Marianne Henry: I am grateful to have you as my ministry partner at *Redeemed Girl*. You are far more than a coworker, you are a precious friend.

To my family: Manonne and Terry, Eric and Muriel, Matt and Marci, and John and Jodi. I am thankful that you are my family but more so that I can call you dear friends. I love you. Thank you Mom and Dad for sacrificially supporting me and loving me the way you do. I am so grateful for all that Jesus has done in our family.

Finally, to my best friend Jesus Christ: You are my life, my joy, and my song. Thank You for the greatest act of friendship of all time; Your death brought me life! Thank You for letting me to be part of *Your* story. I pray this book brings You much glory.

Notes

Chapter 1

1. Gary Thomas, *Holy Available* (Grand Rapids: Zondervan, 2009), 177.

2. An excellent resource for those wanting to learn more about the reliability of Scripture is Erwin Lutzer, *Seven Reasons Why You Can Trust the Bible* (Chicago: Moody Press, 2008). In a society where truth is considered relative, it is of utmost importance that Christians believe absolutely that the Bible is the Word of God.

Chapter 2

1. C. S. Lewis, *The Four Loves*, (New York: Mariner Books, 1971), 96–97.

2. Mark Driscoll, "Proverbs: Friendship," Mars Hill Community Church Seattle Podcast, August 25, 2009. Christians need friends to survive. Pastor Mark Driscoll teaches on the importance of friendships to the Christian in this latest installment of Proverbs.

3. Wayne Martindale and Jerry Root, eds., *The Quotable Lewis*, (Carol Stream, IL: Tyndale House, 1989), entry number 536, p. 238.

4. Les Parrott and Leslie Parrott, *A Good Friend: 10 Traits of Enduring Ties* (Ann Arbor: Vine Books, 1998), 11.

Chapter 3

1. Robert McGee, *The Search for Significance* (Nashville: Thomas Nelson, 1998), 76.
2. Dee Brestin, *The Friendships of Women: The Beauty and Power of God's Plan for Us* (Colorado Springs: David C. Cook, 2008), 226.
3. C. S. Lewis, *The Four Loves*, (New York: Mariner Books, 1971), 96–97.
4. McGee, *The Search for Significance*, 77.
5. Dan Allender and Tremper Longman III, *Breaking the Idols of Your Heart: How to Navigate the Temptations of Life* (Downers Grove: IVP Books, 2007), 59.
6. Ibid., 60.

Chapter 4

1. Joy Carroll, *The Fabric of Friendship: Celebrating the Joys, Mending the Tears in Women's Relationships* (Notre Dame, IN: Sorin Books, 2006), 56, 58.
2. Ibid., 58.
3. Rosalind Wieseman, *Queen Bees and Wannabees: Helping Your Daughter Survive Cliques, Gossip, Boyfriends, and Other Realities of Adolescence* (New York: Three Rivers Press, 2003), 114.

Chapter 5

1. Dan R. Allender, *The Healing Path: How the Hurts in Your Past Can Lead You to a More Abundant Life* (Colorado Springs: WaterBrook Press, 2000), 15.
2. Sandra D. Wilson, *Hurt People Hurt People* (Grand Rapids: Discovery House Publishers, 2001), 12.
3. Ibid., 9–10.
4. Brenda Hunter, *In the Company of Women: Deepening Our Relationships with the Important Women in Our Lives* (Colorado Springs: Multnomah, 1994) as quoted in Paula Rineheart, *Strong Women Soft Hearts: A Woman's Guide to Cultivating a Wise Heart and a Passionate Life* (Nashville: Thomas Nelson, 2005), 117.

Chapter 6

1. Les Parrott and Leslie Parrott, *A Good Friend: 10 Traits of Enduring Ties* (Ann Arbor: Vine Books, 1998), 83.
2. Alan Loy McGinnis, *The Friendship Factor: How to Get Closer to People You Care For* (Minneapolis: Augsburg, 2004), 33.
3. Ibid., 22.
4. Irene S. Levine, *Best Friends Forever: Surviving a Breakup with Your Best Friend* (New York: Overlook Press, 2009), 142.
5. McGinnis, *The Friendship Factor*, 16.
6. Parrott and Parrott, *A Good Friend*, 18.
7. Ibid., 74.
8. Erin Smalley and Carrie Oliver, *Grown-Up Girlfriends: Finding and Keeping Real Friends in the Real World* (Carol Stream, IL: Tyndale House, 2007), 140.
9. Ibid., 136.

Chapter 7

1. C. S. Lewis, *The Four Loves*, (New York: Mariner Books, 1971), 97.
2. Wayne Martindale and Jerry Root, eds., *The Quotable Lewis* (Carol Stream, IL: Tyndale House, 1989), entry number 523, p. 233.

MORE BOOKS BY
MARIAN JORDAN